Tax Guide 203

STARTING
YOUR
BUSINESS

by

Holmes F. Crouch
Tax Specialist

Published by

Allyear Tax Guides

**20484 Glen Brae Drive
Saratoga, CA 95070**

ISBN 0-944817-51-3

LCCN 98-70246

Printed in U.S.A.

Series 200
Investors & Businesses

Tax Guide 203

STARTING YOUR BUSINESS

For other titles in print, see page 224.

The author: **Holmes F. Crouch**
For more about the author, see page 221.

PREFACE

If you are a knowledge-seeking **taxpayer** looking for information, this book can be helpful to you. It is designed to be read — from cover to cover — in less than eight hours. Or, it can be "skim-read" in about 30 minutes.

Either way, you are treated to **tax knowledge** . . . *beyond the ordinary*. The "beyond" is that which cannot be found in IRS publications, FedWorld on-line services, tax software programs, or on CD-ROMs.

Taxpayers have different levels of interest in a selected subject. For this reason, this book starts with introductory fundamentals and progresses onward. You can verify the progression by chapter and section in the table of contents. In the text, "applicable law" is quoted in pertinent part. Key phrases and key tax forms are emphasized. Real-life examples are given . . . in down-to-earth style.

This book has 12 chapters. This number provides depth without cross-subject rambling. Each chapter starts with a head summary of meaningful information.

To aid in your skim-reading, informative diagrams and tables are placed strategically throughout the text. By leafing through page by page, reading the summaries and section headings, and glancing at the diagrams and tables, you can get a good handle on the matters covered.

Effort has been made to update and incorporate all of the latest tax law changes that are *significant* to the title subject. However, "beyond the ordinary" does not encompass every conceivable variant of fact and law that might give rise to protracted dispute and litigation. Consequently, if a particular statement or paragraph is crucial to your own specific case, you are urged to seek professional counseling. Otherwise, the information presented is general and is designed for a broad range of reader interests.

The Author

INTRODUCTION

When we say "Starting Your Business," we are referring to a small business. By "small" we mean an active business whose gross receipts for a given year are less than $1,000,000.

For a business of less than $1,000,000 it is impractical to hire tax accountants and tax attorneys on a full-time basis. Although tax consultants may be employed from time to time, by and large the owners of a startup business have to carry the tax burden on their own. Therefore, it is the persons involved in starting a small business towards whom this book is intended.

There are five ways to start a small business. You can—

1.   Inherit it from close family,
2.   Buy an existing business,
3.   Franchise into a business,
4.   Spin off from a larger business,
5.   Start from scratch on your own.

Once you are in business, how you got started is rather immaterial. Your ongoing operational activities are unrelated to your prebusiness acquisition options.

You have a choice in the *form* of business that you start with. You can choose to be a proprietorship, a partnership, or a corporation. Each form has its own advantages and disadvantages. We'll explain the differences in appropriate chapters in this book.

Whatever initial form you choose, your decision is not forever cast in concrete. You can always change your form of business at any time. Yes, of course, there are procedures to follow when selecting your initial form, and there are procedures to follow when changing your initial form. Whatever form you choose, you should not do so based on any misperceived tax or legal benefits. As the business owner, you are always liable for the tax misdeeds and mismanagement activities that take place during your course of operation.

Upon starting, every business, large or small, will face recurring demands by government taxing agencies. But a small business will encounter these demands more persistently and more aggressively than a large business. There is a simple reason for this. A small business is easier to target than a large business. Tax targeting by government agencies is time consuming, energy draining, income depleting, and — above all — a major distraction from the purpose and thrust of the intended business. We hope to give you some forming-good-habit guidelines for at least minimizing these tax drains.

Other than gross mismanagement, tax mismanagement is one of the greatest causes of new business failures. Many a new business has been abruptly shut down by Big Brother: The Internal Revenue Service (IRS). Most of these shutdowns are for failure to file employer tax returns, and/or for failure to withhold and pay quarterly income tax withholdings, social security taxes, medicare taxes, and federal unemployment taxes. We devote a whole chapter to these employer tax matters. What we are trying to tell you now is that *tax matters* should be among your foremost concerns when starting any new business.

Your very first tax-matter concern is: what to do about startup costs. As we all know, starting any new business requires certain up-front expenditures. One must spend money for investigating, creating, and bringing into operation an active trade or business. Taxwise, how do you handle these up-front expenditures?

Answer: You can *not* deduct them currently.

Why not?

Because Section 195 of the Internal Revenue Code (**Start-up Expenditures**) says—

> *(a) Capitalization of Expenditures*
> *Except as otherwise provided in this section, no deduction shall be allowed for start-up expenditures.*

This seems pretty clear. "No deduction shall be allowed" (period). This means that your startup costs must be capitalized and treated as part of your tax basis when the business is sold, abandoned, or otherwise terminated.

Taxwise, you are not in business until the first dollar of income is derived from a product or service when offered to the general public. Purchases by family members and close friends do not count. That first dollar of income must come from some unrelated party in the public at large. And, following this first dollar, there must be some expectation that your business will be ongoing and active. From this point on, you are "in business."

CONTENTS

1

PREBUSINESS MATTERS

Every "Trade Or Business" Has A Tax Definition Of Its Own. Foremost Is A Profit Motive With Substantial Participation By The Owner(s) Therein. Otherwise, Not-For-Profit Rules And Passive Activity Rules Come Into Play. Having More than One Business Is Tax Suspect If One Is Successful And The Others Are Not. Until Your New Business Is Active And Ongoing, It Is A "Nonbusiness." It May Take Several Years To Get Started. During This Time, Accumulate Systematically Your Investigatory And Physical Asset Costs. Later, The Investigatory Costs Can Be "Amortized," And The Physical Assets "Depreciated."

Every new business starts with a bright idea in someone's fertile mind. Bringing this idea into fruition takes time, effort, and capital (money). Although many bright ideas can form in one's mind, only those which culminate into an active trade or business are recognized for tax purposes. All other ideas are just passing thoughts in an ongoing dream world.

The time, effort, and money between the idea and its germination is referred to as the *prebusiness phase* of a business. As we indicated in the Introduction, this is the phase in which there are no tax benefits whatsoever. If the new business never comes to fruition, all expenditures incurred are treated as nondeductible personal expenses. They are personal because they originate in one's mind. They are nondeductible because there is no business income against which such expenditures can be allocated.

It is important, therefore, that we touch on various matters that you should know about, before your business gets going. To do this, we will focus more on how a tax agency looks at your business rather than on what your thoughts might be. Although the Internal Revenue Service itself is not a business (it is a federal bureaucracy), it has a lot to say about what constitutes your business.

"Trade or Business" Defined

Throughout the Internal Revenue Code, the phrase "trade or business" frequently appears. This raises the logical question: What is a trade or business? How is it defined?

In essence, a trade or business is an activity carried on for profit. Underlying everything else, there must be a true and genuine profit-seeking motive. While there can never be a guarantee of profit, there must be a reasonable expectation of earning one, under ordinary market conditions. If the profit motive is lacking, the activity is a not-for-profit endeavor. Such endeavors are not tax recognized.

Tax recognition arises from the fact that when a profit is made, there are taxes to be paid. Tax agencies simply will not recognize your business unless there is government revenue to be derived.

Associated with the profit motive of a business, is the earning of a livelihood by the owner or owners thereof. One cannot earn a livelihood if the business loses money year after year. Therefore, when a profit is made, there are taxes to pay. The after-tax profit is thus available for sustaining the livelihood and well-being of the entrepreneur(s) involved.

A profit is made when a product or service is offered on an ongoing basis. The term "ongoing" means: day-to-day, month-to-month, year-to-year. In other words, a one-time profit does not constitute a business. More likely than not, a one-time profit is either an investment, a wager, a hobby, a recreation, or other personal transaction. To be recognized as a trade or business, the profit must be made on a continuing and repeated basis. In the continuum process, some of the transactions may be made at a profit, and some may be made at a loss. The vicissitudes of the marketplace determine the net profitability . . . or net loss.

Another feature of a trade or business is the offering of your product or service to the general public. While the form of ownership may be private, the business must be open to the public at large. Family members, close friends, business associates, and others in exclusionary groupings do not constitute the general public. While a net profit may indeed be made from such persons, the transactions are suspect. This is because the element of competition is lacking.

At this point, we have described four essential features that characterize a trade or business (for tax purposes). There is a fifth feature — material participation — that we must tell you about separately.

Material Participation Required

In 1986, Congress passed many new tax laws affecting small businesses. Some of the new laws are "anti" small business in the sense that they redefine what a trade or business is. The particular new law on point is Section 469: *Passive Activity Losses Limited.* In essence, Section 469 classifies a trade or business into two categories. These two categories are (1) a *passive activity* business, and (2) a *material participation* business.

A passive activity business is one where the conduct of the owner(s) does not qualify it as a material participation business. The passive activity owner(s) are overseers and investors. They are more interested in the generation of tax benefits rather than in the day-to-day operation of the business. A discussion of passive activity businesses is beyond the scope of this book. Our focus is solely on material participation businesses.

A material participation business is one in which the owner or owners are involved in the business operations on a regular, continuous, and substantial basis. This level of participation must be maintained throughout the tax year. Included in this feature is participation of the owner's spouse, where appropriate. A husband and wife in business together are treated as one taxpayer.

A taxpayer is most likely to have participated where his own involvement is his principal activity. In other words, his primary income depends on the success of the business. By contrast, a full-time lawyer or doctor who invests in an orange grove is unlikely to have materially participated in the orange grove business. Their money participates, but not their persons.

A "highly relevant" factor is how regularly you as owner are present at the place where your principal business operations are carried on. Full-time involvement is not necessary if the nature of the business is seasonal, or where qualified employees and independent contractors perform designated routine and special tasks. In other words, being at your place of business 8 to 10 hours each day is not crucial. You are materially participating if you do everything that is required to conduct and control the business.

To summarize where we are at this point, we present Figure 1.1. We identify therein the five key elements for gaining tax recognition as a trade or business. But, as we will see below, even full compliance with Figure 1.1 provides no tax guarantees.

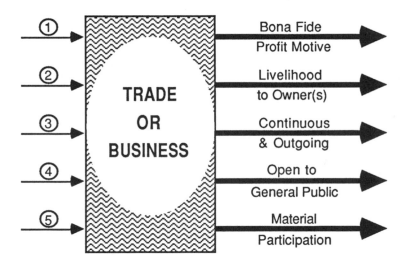

Fig. 1.1 - Tax Essentials of a Trade or Business

The Not-for-Profit Presumption

Government always has a lot to say about how you run your business. It can't run its own affairs properly, but it can tell you how to run yours. As far as profit-making is concerned, the government — via the IRS — says that you must make a profit in any three out of five consecutive years that you are in business. If you do not make such a profit, it is *presumed* that you are engaged in a not-for-profit activity.

This is all spelled out in tax code Section 183: *Activities Not Engaged in for Profit.* The essence of this tax law is that—

> *In the case of an activity . . . not engaged in for profit, no deduction attributable to such activity shall be allowed . . . except . . . to the extent [of] the gross income derived from such activity for the taxable year.*

Let us exemplify what this means. Suppose that the gross income from your business is $10,000 for the year. To derive this amount, you actually spent $30,000. According to Section 183, you have a $20,000 personal loss which is not tax recognized. It is a "loss-loss."

This is the old familiar story encountered by experienced persons in business. If the flip of a coin comes up "heads" — the government wins. If it comes up "tails" — the government also wins. In either case, it is a loss-loss to you.

The teeth of Section 183 are found in subsection (d): Presumption. This subsection reads in part—

> *If the gross income derived from an activity for 3 or more of the taxable years in the period of 5 consecutive taxable years . . . exceeds the deductions attributable to such activity . . . then, unless the [IRS] establishes to the contrary, such activity shall be presumed . . . to be an activity engaged in for profit.*

Thus, the reverse presumption is that if you do not make a profit in three out of five years, you are some kind of flake trying to rip off the government. As a tax "presumption," however, you can refute this anti-business stance of the IRS.

In more specific terms, IRS Regulation 1.183-2(a) says—

> *For purposes of Section 183 . . . the term "activity not engaged in for profit" means any activity . . . carried on primarily as a sport, hobby, or for recreation. The determination . . . is to be made by reference to objective standards, taking into account all of the facts and circumstances of each case. Although a reasonable expectation of profit is not required, the facts and circumstances must indicate that the taxpayer entered into the*

activity, or continued the activity, **with the objective of making a profit.** [Emphasis supplied.]

So the key for distinguishing between for-profit and not-for-profit is the *objective* of making a profit. In determining whether this objective exists, the amount of profit is immaterial. Whether small or large, the objective exists if there is a reasonable chance of making some profit. Greater weight is given to objective facts rather than to one's mere statement of intent.

Nine Objective Factors

Not many businesses make a significant profit in the first few years of operation. Startup losses are the rule rather than the exception. Consequently, the first few years of a new trade or business are the most vulnerable to IRS attack. This is particularly true if the loss claimant has other sources of positive income.

In Regulation 1.183-2(b), the IRS has set forth nine different relevant factors for determining whether a business is operated for profit. These nine factors are identified in Figure 1.2. Note that a thumbnail description of each factor is presented. We also show checkboxes for entering "Yes" or "No" when reviewing your own business activity. A "Yes" means for profit whereas a "No" means not-for-profit.

The listing in Figure 1.2 is not all inclusive. Depending on the particular business that you envision, there may be other factors that should be considered. No one factor in Figure 1.2 is determinative by itself. Nor, as the IRS says, is a determination to be made on the basis that the number of factors indicating a profit motive exceeds the number of factors indicating a lack of profit objective. In other words, Figure 1.2 is not a scoreboard for determining whether the number of "Yes's" exceeds the number of "No's."

The manner of carrying on a business (Factor 1 in Figure 1.2) is certainly one good indication of the "Yes" or "No" profit motive. If the owner carries on his affairs in a businesslike manner, and he keeps complete and accurate books and records, he certainly has a profit objective in mind. Similarly, where an activity is carried on in a manner comparable to competitive activities of the same nature which are profitable, a profit motive may be indicated.

On the other hand, if there are elements of personal pleasure or recreation which stand out (Factor 9 in Figure 1.2), a not-for-profit objective is suspected. Apparently, one is not supposed to enjoy or

Tax Test	ITEM	DESCRIPTION	Yes	No
1.	Manner of conducting business	Businesslike with complete and accurate records; changing unprofitable methods and improving operations.		
2.	Expertise of owner and advisors	Adequate preparation, research, study, and follow-through with sound "business plan"; pursuing new products and services.		
3.	Time and effort expended by owners	Devotion of much time and energy to an activity where personal and recreational aspects are minimal.		
4.	Expectation of growth and appreciation	Current profits not determinative if prospects of business growth and appreciation of assets are realistic.		
5.	Success in other similar activities	Prior business success and turn-arounds indicative of of profit making intent in current business.		
6.	History of losses and reasons therefor	Continued losses must be explainable in terms of risks, reverses, unforseens, and depressed markets.		
7.	Occaisionality of profits: some large, some small	With large capital involved, irregular profits indicate speculative venture with chance to make big.		
8.	Other sources of income	If primary income from current activity: good; if substantial other income: bad.		
9.	Elements of personal pleasure or recreation	Particularly suspect are activities involving sports, hobbies, entertainment, collector items, exotic pets, and prestigiousness.		

Fig. 1.2 - Factors Indicating a "For Profit" Activity

like his work. The inference is that one must work with the exclusive intention of deriving a profit . . . and maximizing it. However, the fact that one does derive some personal pleasure from his business is not, in and of itself, determinative, if the for-profit objective is evidenced by other factors.

More Than One Business

Having more than one business tends to be tax suspect. This is especially true where one business is highly successful and the other is not. The passive loss rules and the not-for-profit rules both come into play.

For example, suppose you own and run business A and business B. Business A is highly successful: your net profit is $100,000 year after year. But business B is a loser. Its net loss year after year is $35,000. As the common owner of both businesses, you can net-net the $100,000 profit with the $35,000 loss. This gives you a taxable net of $65,000. In a situation like this, you can be sure that — at some point in time — business B will be tax scrutinized.

There is nothing inherently wrong with having two, three, or more businesses. Nor is there anything wrong with one or more being successful, and one or more being unsuccessful. That is, there is nothing wrong so long as there is a clear business purpose and rationale for each business. Each business should be a separate economic unit, separately managed with separate record-keeping, and targeting separate segments of the public marketplace.

Where there is common ownership of more than one business, the test of *economic reality* applies. Do the separate businesses complement each other in a seasonal and functional manner, which makes good business sense? Or, does one of them appear to be a "front" or tax shelter for the main business of the owner(s)?

Here's an example of economic reality involving three separate businesses. You and your spouse own a motel which produces good net income. The peak season, however, is June through September, which is four months of the year. What do you do during the eight months of off-season?

Suppose you have background and training in commercial advertising. You start an advertising business whose peak season is October through January (four months). Suppose your spouse has a background in geography and travel. She starts a small travel agency whose peak season for bookings and reservations is

February through May (four months). Together, you have three separate businesses. Each is a separate economic unit; each offers a different product or service; and each has a separate niche in the marketplace. Nothing is tax-wrong with this at all . . . providing you keep *separate* books and records for each business.

On the other hand, suppose you inherit a large farm, but you work in the city on a full-time basis. You pay someone to manage and run the farm. As most farms do, it produces a loss year after year. Now, farming is a perfectly legitimate business for one who indeed "works the land." Since you don't work the land, you are a gentleman farmer. Gentleman farming is not a trade or business. Hence, the not-for-profit rules apply.

Methods & Phases of "Starting"

What is a new business, and when does it start? It is "new" in the sense that you as the owner have never operated that business before. It "starts" when you are prepared to follow through on your first public offering of a product or service . . . which is accepted. Up to the point where an active/ongoing enterprise begins to take shape, you are *not* in business.

One can start a new business in any of several ways. You can start from scratch. You can inherit a business or gradually buy into one. You can revive a defunct business. You can acquire a business by purchase or by franchising. Or, you can spin off a new business from an existing business in which you have participated.

Rather than discussing each of the ways of getting started, we present a brief summary of their pros and cons in Figure 1.3. Our position is that no matter how you actually get started, there is a prebusiness phase of thinking and planning. You just don't jump into business overnight.

For any of the starting methods in Figure 1.3, there are five stages of entry progression. In sequential order, these stages are:

I— The Prerequisite Stage

• You must have some prior knowledge, experience, background, or training in the new business line that you expect to engage in. You should also have some foreknowledge of the specific product(s) and/or service(s) that you intend to offer, in your target market domain.

METHOD	PROS	CONS
1. Inheriting from parent(s) or close family	Established product, service, market, & clients; long track record of earnings; ongoing goodwill makes take-over easy.	Long "estate transfer" period; product/service may be out-of date; inheritor may be disinterested in continuing the business.
2. Buying (or buying into) existing business	Good growth potential if business on sound footing; saves trial and error; earnings record & marketing can be examined.	Might just be buying prior owner(s)' problems; all facts may not be fully disclosed; probably near defunct or near retirement.
3. Franchising into a national product/service	Proven product or service line "nationally advertised"; management training provided; products delivered without credit hassle.	Large amount of entry capital needed; franchisor may set unrealistic sales goals; difficult to change product or service line.
4. "Spin-off" from successful larger business	Long "incubation time" to assess new product/service; some financial assistance; temporary sharing of facilities.	Requires covenants "not-to-compete"; covenants against "raiding" of personnel; potential lawsuits over patent and market infringements.
5. Starting new from scratch; "bootstrapping"	If unique product or service, can be "highly satisfying"; complete ownership and control; no covenants or prior lines to continue.	Initial "floundering" can be costly; endangered competition can be ruthless; repeat customers & clients slow to develop.

Fig. 1.3 - Ways Of Getting Started in Business

II— The Idea Formulation Stage

• An incubation period of reading, talking, thinking, and investigating the new venture that you are about to embark on; the idea needs to become a reality in your mind and not just a passing dream. To test your idea, engage in informal discussions with prospective customers, clients, and your friends.

III— The Paper Plan Stage

• Here is where you write it all down: charts, diagrams, and outlines; you define your "business objectives": your product or service, marketing strategy, "marketing plan," production and/or supply sources, and the organizational personnel that you will need.

IV— The Earnest Money Stage

• Up-front money has to be expended for inventory, materials, supplies, equipment, rental space, utilities, consultants, and contractors; who will advance this money . . . and how much is needed?

V— The First Offering Stage

• Detailed preparatory effort in the form of contracts, commitments, advertising, promotion, name recognition, address, hours of operation, and so on; guarantee of delivery and follow-through.

Stages I though III should be on a very low budget. The planning and formulation of a new business idea requires more time and thought than it does money. Doing things on paper is much cheaper than doing them in fact. Beginner mistakes can be made which can be corrected before serious money is committed. Research, phone calls, and perhaps a short trip or two, are not high-cost items. Absorb these costs in your personal budget. Don't even bother to keep record of them. They are — or should be — rather trivial when compared to the costs in Stages IV and V.

Startup Costs Defined

In the sequential listing above, stages IV and V are where the serious money is needed. Every proposed venture has to undergo some prebusiness expenditures to bring the concept into a form conducive to public acceptance. Make sure that you have enough money and resources to do this. Most new businesses fail at this point (called: *undercapitalization*). At this point, also, serious record-keeping must commence.

The costs in stages IV and V can be segregated into two classifications: *intangible* costs and *tangible* costs. Intangible costs are those incurred for the investigative, creative, organizational, consultative, and promotional aspects of getting a business going. Tangible costs, on the other hand, are those incurred for the acquisition of vehicles, machinery, equipment, furniture, and fixtures — physical assets — to be used in the business. Separate record-keeping should be maintained for each of these two classes of expenditures.

Tax code Section 195(c) defines "start-up expenditures" as—

Any amount . . . paid or incurred in connection with—
(i) investigating the creation or acquisition of an active trade or business, or
(ii) creating an active trade or business, or
(iii) any activity engaged in for profit and for the production of income before the day on which the active trade or business begins.

If you read this section carefully, you will see that no distinction is made between intangible (nonphysical) and tangible (physical) costs. You are left out on a limb. Section 195(c) is trying to tell you just one thing. All expenditures incurred before a business actually begins must be accumulated separately from the business itself. If the intended business never gets going, these accumulated costs are not tax recognized. No income has been generated against which they can be deducted.

If your business indeed gets going, then the distinction between intangible and tangible costs becomes important. Intangible costs can be amortized (Sec. 195(b)); tangible costs can be depreciated (Sec. 167(a)). We will reserve to a later chapter all discussion on amortization and depreciation. These become "spread-out" deductions against the income of the active business.

Simplified Cost Accumulation

Very few new businesses actually start up and get going within a given tax year. Usually, two, three, or more preparatory years are involved. During this time, you will be incurring costs which have no immediate benefit to you. Chances are, you'll become cavalier about these costs. You'll either try to write them off against other sources of income, or you may overlook them altogether.

You may even have several new business ideas in your mind all at one time. Your style may be to trial-and-error each one until one of them clicks. Obviously, you need some sort of systematic cost accumulation system.

The minute you start spending real money, we urge that you establish a "business startup" checking account. Do this at the financial institution of your choice. Use your personal name and the personal name(s) of your associate(s). Do not use any fictitious name nor any prospective business name. Up to the point where your prospective business actually goes into operation, all of the expenditures are essentially personal.

What is "real money" to justify setting up a separate startup checking account? That depends on the nature and capital requirements of your proposed business. Certainly, if your cumulative costs begin to exceed $1,000, you should open the separate account. Then feed personal money into this account in $1,000 to $10,000 increments, as needed. The deposit confirmation slips become third-party records as to whose personal money was deposited, and how much. Forget about interest on the deposits. The startup account is not for personal savings; it is simply a cost accumulation check-writing system.

We now suggest a really neat feature to you. Have the financial institution print *two* different types of checks: different colors with different imprint designs. Use the same account number and personal names on both checks. All you want is to be able to make a quick eye-distinction between the two check forms. Call one your "A" checks and the other your "B" checks.

Use the "A" checks for your intangible cost expenditures and the "B" checks for your tangible costs (physical assets). Having two types of checks forces you to think, on the spot, in terms of intangible/tangible expenditures. Whether you accumulate your costs over several months or several years, this is all the startup tax accounting that you need. Keep your startup life simple. The scheme that we have in mind is depicted in Figure 1.4.

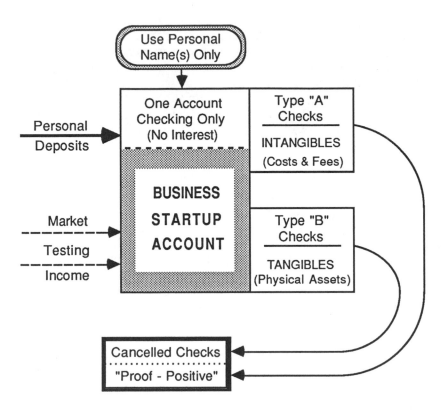

Fig. 1.4- Two-check Accumulation of Startup Costs

When your business finally gets going, you total up all the "A" checks and enter that amount on your tax form amortization schedule. As to the "B" checks, you may have to subcategorize them into vehicles, machinery, equipment, furniture, and fixtures, before entering on your tax form depreciation schedule.

Timing When To Be "In Business"

Every business activity has its own cyclic characteristics: its good months and low months. Consequently, before you make your first offering — your launching experience — you should find out about the seasonal aspects of the business that you are about to enter. Talk to your competition (if you can); talk to friends who are acquainted with the type of business you envision; and talk to potential customers and clients and ascertain their buying habits. Try to determine the best three to five consecutive months of the new business.

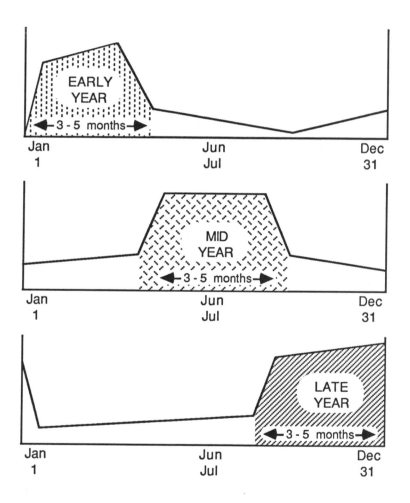

Fig. 1.5 - Likely "Income Profile" of a Small Business

You have spent a wad of personal money getting ready. You don't want to blow it by coming on line off-season. Nor do you want to get in at the very beginning of the next buying season. Existing competition already has the name recognition that you do not have.

The ideal entry timing is approximately one-third of the way into the peak cycle of your intended year. Most customers and clients buy late in the cycle, rather than early. The early buyers habitually go back to their old sources, and rarely try anything new. The mid- and late-cycle buyers are your best chance. Many small businesses have a three- to five-month spread of intense activity, followed by seven to nine months which are slow. In Figure 1.5, we present our depiction of some likely income profiles.

Ideally, you'd like to have a few months after the business cycle wanes to review your launch experience. You want time to critique the affair before you make irreversible decisions. If things look good enough to declare that you are in business, you want time to clean up your act with regard to taxes, licenses, insurance, creditors, complaints, and so forth.

As you know, most tax returns (of all kinds) have to be filed as of the close of the calendar year. Once you file any of these returns as a business, you are locked into a bureaucracy and computer-intimidation system which is difficult to get out of. Therefore, before you get locked in, you want to be sure that you are in business. So, treat your first public offering as a trial balloon. It may turn out that you made a prudent "market test."

During the three to five months' trial experience, there will be income and expenses. If your income exceeds your expenses, you are probably in business. If your expenses exceed income, you have probably made a market test. If a market test, the excess expenses are treated as startup costs. These market testing costs simply add to the cost accumulation system that we presented back in Figure 1.4.

2

SELECTING INITIAL FORM

> There Are Three Basic Forms For Conducting A Business: Proprietorship, Partnership, And Corporation. In Terms Of Ownership And Operation, There Are Advantages And Disadvantages To Each. Tax Differences, However, Are Inconsequential. The Choice Depends On The Nature Of The Business — The Products And/Or Services Offered — And On The Extent Of "Other People's Money" Needed. Your Business Name And Logo Become A "Capital Asset" Which May Increase In Value With Time (Called "Goodwill"). Before Actually Commencing Business, There Is Fictitious Name Publication And Application For Federal I.D. Number.

When starting a business, one common mistake is made. Many entrepreneurs rush off to an attorney and get incorporated. Then they want to set up elaborate pension and profit-sharing plans, plus corporate-paid medical benefits and life insurance. They want to put all of their family autos on the corporate books. They go out and buy a fancy motor home or hot-air balloon (or some other recreational vehicle) and call it the mobile "field office" for their new business.

They do all of these things — or try to — under the illusion that immediate incorporation provides them with magic tax benefits. And they dream of millions of dollars which they can shelter behind the corporate shield, and still have full personal use of the money.

STARTING YOUR BUSINESS

A lot of highly publicized books and seminars seem to emphasize this magic.

Our advice is: DON'T DO IT! Don't rush out to incorporate.

If you do, you are digging yourself *two* graves. You are digging your tax grave, and you are digging your financial grave.

Instead, think of yourself as a little seed being dropped from a high-flying bird. You are dropped randomly onto hostile landscape. Before you as the little seed can become the giant oak tree that you envision, there is a lot of germination, rooting, nutrition, and growth to be achieved. Good implantation requires the right niche, the right environment, the right market, the right economic conditions and — yes — some plain old-fashioned luck.

We don't want you to think small. We just don't want you to think magic. There are a lot of tax wolves out there ready to tear your business apart under the slightest pretext. So, you'd better think slow and methodical.

The Basic Forms of Business

There are three basic forms of doing business. There is the proprietorship form; there is the partnership form; and there is the corporate form. There are hybrids and variants of these three forms, but basically these constitute the more conventionally recognized ways of going into business.

The choice of one business form over another depends on the type of business to be launched. The choice also depends on the customary practices of others in a similar type business. Public expectations play some role, but such role is not absolute. More importantly, the manner of ownership and the financial needs of the emerging business are far more decision controlling.

By far the simplest form of new business is the sole proprietorship. It is simple because there is only one owner: the creator. This one owner may also be a husband and wife. (A husband and wife are treated as one taxpayer: not two.) The startup and follow-through come from the personal savings of the creator, and/or from borrowings from family relations and close friends. Or, equity lines of credit can be set up against other nonbusiness assets of the creator. Whatever the source of money, there is one-owner control over the business. The business succeeds or fails on the expertise, intelligence, and drive of this one owner. He, she, or they accrue all profits . . . and suffer all losses.

A partnership is where two or more owners (with money) get together to share the profits and loss of the business. They are partners in that they are co-owners. This means that they have (essentially) equal say in all transactional decisions. The most successful partnerships involve three principals, each of whom brings a separate yet complementary expertise to the business. Each needs the other, so to speak. Each contributes startup money or the equivalent, though often in unequal amounts. Partnerships tend to lose cohesiveness when the number of general partners reaches five. Person-to-person communication problems develop which can cause breakdown of the partnership.

A corporation is where the business is owned by a group of persons: called shareholders. A small business corporation can consist of five (or fewer) shareholders to as many as 35. The shareholders have "voting power" in proportion to the dollar value of their shares. The shareholders elect a chief executive to run the business, and may also elect other principal operating officers. The officers get a salary for their personal services, whereas the shareholders get a "dividend" if the business succeeds. Corporations, usually, can raise more capital than proprietorships or partnerships.

The point that we are trying to make here is this: The form of business that you select will depend on the number of owners and their contributions of capital. As more owners become involved, operational complexity increases. A one-owner company is more flexible and resilient to change than is a 35-owner company. New businesses are always plagued with unforeseens and the need to change and modify.

While the availability of lots of startup capital is nice, there also can be lots of headaches. Not every new business blooms forth without faltering. The moment any faltering occurs, the money contributors become litigious. They want their money back . . . NOW, or they will sue. Lawsuits can be devastating. Every owner (other than yourself) is always a potential adversary. So, beware of other people's money when starting a brand new business.

Variants and Hybrids Thereof

Often, businesses are organized and operated as variants and hybrids of the three basic forms. Some, but not all, are treated as a trade or business for tax purposes. Furthermore, some of the variants invoke special tax rules which subject them to special treatment by themselves. We want to eliminate all special-type businesses in order to sharpen the focus of our treatment on the basic forms.

For example, there are actually two forms of sole proprietorships. There is the ordinary business form and the farming business form. Farming is the harvesting of sources of food from land and water (fishing). Farming is chronically a loss-type business. It is made viable only through vast government subsidies and special concessions to workers. Moreover, farming is a business usually handed down from generation to generation. It is unlikely to be a venture in which one would start from scratch on his own. Accordingly, we will limit our treatment to ordinary business proprietorships.

As to partnerships, there also are two forms. There is the general partnership and the limited partnership. In a general partnership, all owners are co-liable for the debts of the business without limit. In contrast, in a limited partnership, the limited partners are liable only up to the amount of their capital contributed. As limited partners, they take no active role in the day-to-day affairs of the business. They are primarily passive investors.

Limited partnerships are popular conduits for tax shelter programs. They are "conduits" in the sense that all loss writeoffs and tax credits pass through to the individual limited partners. Because of this pass-through feature, and the passivity of the contributors of capital, the Tax Reform Act of 1986 automatically classifies all limited partnerships as *passive activity* businesses. As such, they are not an active trade or business. Stringent loss limitation and benefit recapture rules apply. Consequently, we dismiss any further discussion on limited partnerships. Our focus is entirely on general (active) partnership forms.

In the corporate domain, there is much more latitude for variants and hybrids. There are two "ordinary business" corporations: the C-type and the S-type. The "S" stands for a small business corporation having not more than 75 shareholders. There are also some 15 "special purpose" type corporations. We will not discuss any of these special purpose corporations. Instead, we list them for you in Figure 2.1 and indicate the tax code sections which address them. Rarely are any of the Figure 2.1 corporations suitable for starting up a new business.

The latest buzz form for new business startups is the Limited Liability Company (LLC). This is a hybrid entity with all the elements of a limited partnership and S-type corporation. An S-

NO.	TYPE	PURPOSE	TAX CODE
1	DISC	Domestic international sales corp.	Sec. 992
2	F	Foreign corporation	Sec. 882
3	FC	Farmer's cooperative	Sec. 1381
4	FPHC	Foreign personal holding company	Sec. 552
5	FSC	Foreign sales corporation	Sec. 922
6	H	Homeowners association	Sec. 528
7	L	Life insurance company	Sec. 801
8	M	Other insurance company	Sec. 831
9	ND	Nuclear decommission trust	Sec. 468A
10	PHC	Personal holding company	Sec. 542
11	POL	Political organization	Sec. 527
12	REIT	Real estate investment trust	Sec. 856
13	REMIC	Real estate mortgage investment co.	Sec. 860A
14	RIC	Regulated investment co.	Sec. 851
15	SBIC	Small business investment co.	Sec. 1242

Fig. 2.1 - Listing of "Special Purpose" Corporations

corporation is a conduit entity in that all income, losses, and credits pass through to the individual shareholders. As such, S-corporations carry a "tax shelter" stigma. But as an LLC, this stigma is removed, and the business can operate similarly to a C-corporation. However, many tax and legal questions arise concerning whether an LLC is a partnership or a corporation, and whether the owners are truly shielded from product and service lawsuits. Much depends on the particular state law under which LLCs and S-corporations are formed.

For purposes of this book, therefore, we will not address further LLCs or S-type corporations. A regular C-type corporation has all of the small business features that you'll ever need.

From this point on, we limit our focus to sole proprietorships (one owner), general partnerships (two to five owners) and regular corporations (five owners or more). Before selecting *your* initial business form, a quick review of the pros and cons of each may be instructive.

Proprietorship Pros and Cons

The primary advantage of a sole proprietorship is that it lends itself to a family operation. Husband, wife, and children can run the business with little outside help from others. All profits from the business accrue to the headmaster (or headmistress) of the family. The wife can be employed by the husband, or vice versa, and the children can be employed by either.

Even though the business may be run by husband and wife jointly, the term "sole proprietorship" means that only one of the spouses can be tax designated as the owner. This is because in a proprietorship, the net profits are subject to self-employment tax (in addition to the regular income tax). If there were two owners of the business each tax identified, there would be two self employment taxes to pay. So, there is an advantage in having only one of the spouses designated as the owner.

If the husband is the owner, he can employ his wife in the business. Whether he pays her wages or not depends on their working relationship, their handling of finances, and whether the wife wants a separate social security earnings record of her own. If wages are paid, the husband is subject to all of the same employer taxes and withholdings of a giant corporation. This means two social security/medicare taxes to pay: his and hers. If the spouses have been — or plan to be — married more than ten years, the wife will get 50% of her husband's social security benefits . . . without paying any wages to her.

Wages paid to children employed by their parents are exempt from the social security tax. This exemption, however, applies only up to the age of 18. After this age, the parents must withhold the social security tax on all wages paid. In most cases, after — and often before — reaching age 18, the children no longer want to work for their parents. Meanwhile, they will have received valuable business training which can be helpful to them in the outside world.

There is one principal disadvantage to a proprietorship. If the tax owner becomes disabled or dies, the business generally goes downhill. Customers who like doing business with the husband and wife start drifting away. They go to other similar husband and wife businesses. In a compatible marriage, a husband and wife in business portray a certain "accommodating balance" towards their customers. This customer balance is difficult to maintain alone by the ongoing spouse.

For summary and check-list purposes, other advantages and disadvantages of a proprietorship are presented in Figure 2.2.

Partnership Pros and Cons

A partnership is the relationship between two or more persons who join together to carry on a trade or business. Each person contributes to the relationship money, property, labor, or skill with the expectation that each will share in the profits and losses of the business. Because of the mixture of money, property, talent, and time available, a partnership is able to extend the scope and depth of its business considerably beyond that of a proprietorship.

The mixture of partner contributions to the business can be any arrangement agreed to between the persons involved. The agreement preferably should be in writing, and signed by all partners. The partners can share equally or unequally in the profits and losses, so long as there is an enforceable contract under local law. This provides great flexibility to the business to meet changing economic conditions. Although the partners may share unequally in the "bottom line," they generally share (more or less) equally in the management of the business. This encourages balance, foresight, and compromise which is essential to success in any business.

Once formed in writing, a partnership becomes an *entity* separate and apart from its individual members. Within this entity, a separate "capital account" for each partner is maintained. Thus, each partner can add to, or withdraw from, his own capital account. The conditions for doing so usually are set forth in the partnership agreement. Contributions and withdrawals will change the ownership mix of the entity with the passing of time.

The main disadvantage of a partnership is that each member is personally liable for all debts of the partnership, should other members fail to live up to their agreement. This is called "joint and several liability." Many a conscientious partner has been stuck with all the business debts — including taxes — of his associates, long

PROPRIETORSHIP			
ADVANTAGES		**DISADVANTAGES**	
1.	Simple one-man (or one-woman) business; one owner; one decision maker (includes spouse).	1.	Financial resources limited; equity loan(s) on personal residence often needed.
2.	Can use own true name, followed by DBA (doing business as); register fictitious name(s) with county clerk.	2.	Many a 12-15 hour work day during peak season; if spouse non active, is difficult to get "substitute" manager.
3.	No written documentation required; can start, stop, change nature of business without giving official notice.	3.	Lawsuits can endanger entire personal estate; wild allegations when no written contracts to be interpreted.
4.	Can operate out of own home or garage to cut overhead; business sign not needed if large address numbers displayable.	4.	Zoning ordinances may restrict "in-home" businesses, if delivery trucks, auto parking, and walk-in traffic troublesome.
5.	Can employ own children, neighbors children, friends, & part-time "independent contractors".	5.	Teenagers and part-time help not always reliable; owner subject to penalties if part-timers seek unemployment & social security benefits.
6.	Net profits of the business shared with no one but the owner (and his / her spouse).	6.	Net earnings potential rather limited; other than certain professions, rarely can earnings exceed $100,000.

Fig. 2.2 - Other Pros & Cons of a Proprietorship

after a partnership has broken up. Partnerships tend to break up rapidly when there are downturns in business.

Another disadvantage of partnerships is spousal interferences. Partnership accounting rules and taxation matters are quite different from ordinary wage earner situations. Oftentimes, a partner has to pay income tax on money that he does not actually receive. Some taxable money has to stay in the business to keep operations going, pay employees, buy inventory, get new equipment, maintain lines of credit, and so on. For spouses who are not active in the business themselves, this is difficult to understand. Such spouses also view their partner's capital account as another (federally insured) depository account which can be withdrawn — or borrowed against — at will. The minute that a partner's spouse or other family member begins making financial demands on the partnership, trouble brews. Inevitably, bickering among the partners grows, and soon the business fails.

For summary and check-list purposes, other advantages and disadvantages of a partnership are presented in Figure 2.3. A well-structured partnership can go beyond the disability or death of any partner. This is because a *partnership interest* — as determined by each partner's capital account — is a capital asset. It can be sold or transferred to another person, or it can be bought out by the partnership.

Corporation Pros and Cons

A corporation is a formal entity created under state law. It is formal in the sense that the names of the principals have to be recorded with state authorities, and the articles of incorporation have to be on public file. There is an incorporation fee and an annual continuation fee (nothing to do with taxes). The fee is based on initial capitalization of the corporation and any subsequent changes thereto. Once incorporated, the entity has "indefinite life" . . . until legally dissolved.

Depending on its registration status, a corporation can have any number of owners (shareholders) that it wishes. This affords access to substantial sums of "other people's money." Because of the potential prestige and excitement, investors are more attracted to corporate entities than to noncorporate businesses.

A corporation with five or fewer owners is called a "closely-held" corporation. One with six to 35 owners is called a "private or restricted" entity. When there are more than 35 owners, the corporation acquires a "public entity" status.

The designation of "small" or "large" corporation does not arise from its number of owners, but from its gross sales. In the corporate world, a small business is one whose gross sales are less than $100,000,000 (100 million) in a given year. Really large corporations generate annual sales in excess of $1,000,000,000 (one billion). Our position is that unless your gross sales are

PARTNERSHIP	
ADVANTAGES	**DISADVANTAGES**
1. Near-ideal for 3 to 5 principals whose individual talents complement each other; co-equality in management decisions.	1. If one or more partners start "slacking off" or "overdraw" their capital accounts, serious bickering and mistrust develops.
2. Written "partnership agreement" can be prepared without ratification by government agency; all parties co-sign in presence of each other.	2. Initial agreement is seldom updated, amended, or modified as relationships in business unfold; reality enters and lawsuits often follow.
3. More resources available; partners can contribute any mix of money, property, skill, & labor for which agreed values can be assigned.	3. Where other than money is contributed, "capital accounting" poses severe problems when non-monetary contributors seek "draw down" of their accounts.
4. Principal place of business can be rented in commercial area & paid secretary hired; partners can work out of their own home(s) using their own cars.	4. Commercial space rental often requires long-term leases with penalties for premature termination; workers "play" when the boss is away.
5. Business property such as machinery, equipment, furniture, fixtures, leases, franchises, covenants have "pass-through" benefits to individual partners.	5. Because of diversity of individual partner interests, accurate & stringent record keeping is required; poor records invite intra-partner controversies.
6. Can avoid permanent employees by hiring a "temporary service" agency to supply workers as needed; maximizes pension & profit sharing benefits to partners.	6. Workers with families seek income security with fringe benefits; they accept temporary employment as "last resort"; they tend to be unhappy... always looking elsewhere.

Fig.2.3 - Other Pros & Cons of a Partnership

expected to exceed $1,000,000 in your opening year, it is best not to incorporate initially.

Corporations tend to be more lawsuit prone by customers and clients. Product or service warranties, whether written or implied, are construed as unlimited licenses to raid corporate treasuries. In a real knockdown dragout lawsuit, the imaginary corporate shield provides little or no protection to the officers who run the business. Tax agencies, particularly, can pierce the shield with ease. And so, too, can certain creditors and customers. The idea of incorporating for protecting yourself against tax and legal liability is a myth.

As a summary and check-list, other advantages and disadvantages of a corporation are presented in Figure 2.4. There is one very practical feature of a corporation. It can be sold or redeemed in parts and pieces (shares), without disrupting the continuity of the business. On the other hand, if the business fails, you cannot close the doors and walk away. It has to be legally dissolved. This takes time . . . and more money.

Tax Differences Inconsequential

In our discussions above, we purposely omitted any comparison of the tax benefits of one business form over another. The general impression seems to be that there are more tax benefits in corporate form than in noncorporate form. This is *not true* today.

Commencing in 1976 and extending through 1996, tax law changes have reduced almost to nil any tax benefit differences between business forms. All businesses have to prepare a profit and loss tax statement each year. Items treated as income are the same. Items treated as cost of goods sold are the same. Employer tax matters are the same. Deductible expenses — operational costs, depreciation, travel and entertainment, contract services, employee wages, materials and supplies — are the same. With the only exception of some "fringes" for corporations, the tax rules for determining profit and loss are identical.

As the owner of a business, you are probably more interested in pension and profit-sharing plans for yourself and co-owners. In the past, this was the key element in selecting one business form over another. But no more. Today, each active owner in a business can contribute to his own pension and profit-sharing plan the *lesser* of—

(a) $30,000 per year, or
(b) 25% of his compensation.

CORPORATION	
ADVANTAGES	**DISADVANTAGES**
1. Has potential access to substantial amounts of "other people's money"; 5 to 50 shareholders practical for "small" corporation.	1. Legal registration of stock required; capitalization fees imposed; legal protections to shareholders; not practical if gross sales less than $1,000,000.
2. Board of directors appoints principal operating officers; officers can be changed without jeopardizing policies and objectives.	2. Directors "minutes" required; written policies & procedures required; salaries & perks "highly concentrated" at the top; invites tax attack.
3. Has potential of "indefinite life"; this fosters long range marketing plans & new product development; attracts new capital.	3. If business unsuccessful, cannot simply "walk away"; product liabilities and service warranties must be honored; attracts lawsuits & high "damage awards".
4. Except if "closely-held", shareholders are not active participants; this frees management to devote its "best effort" towards success.	4. All tax, accounting, & financial affairs far more complex; officer-owners often mix personal interest with corporate interests.
5. A more acceptable form of business for intra-state, interstate, & international trade; growth "potentially" unlimited.	5. As markets expand, so do all the problems; internal corruption & bureaucracy grows; necessitates greater expertise of personnel.
6. More attractive to high calibre employees seeking careers & professional development; also fosters "spin-off" businesses.	6. Employees want pay raises, bonuses, fringe benefits, pension & profit sharing plans; overhead costs mount & can get out of control.

Fig. 2.4 - Other Pros & Cons of a Corporation

From his pension and profit-sharing arrangement, the *benefits received* cannot exceed the lesser of—
(1) $90,000 per year (indexed to inflation), or
(2) 100% of the average compensation for his highest three consecutive years of plan participation.

Except for some technical differences, these overall limits apply to proprietorships, partnerships, and corporations alike.

In the fringe benefit area (medical coverage, group life insurance, educational assistance, company car, travel reimbursement, and so on) there is still a slight edge in corporate form. But for a small business just getting started, all fringes are a financial burden on limited resources. Furthermore, if the owners receive fringes more favorable than their employees, the owners have to pay taxes on their fringes. There has been an ongoing evolution of stringent nondiscrimination fringe-benefit rules being enacted.

The use of a company car is now a tax nightmare. If the car is used by an owner for any personal use such as commuting or on week-ends, the personal use portion has to be valued. Said value is then added to his taxable compensation. If the company car is leased, an "annual lease value" is added to taxable compensation. For example, a $35,000 auto has a taxable lease value of $9,250 [as per Reg. 1.61-21(d)(2)(iii)]. Adding this amount to an owner's compensation forces him to keep accurate record of his true business mileage, which is deductible.

Travel and entertainment rules, including meals and lodging, have been tightened severely. Written company policies must be established; expenses must be adequately substantiated; and there must be a clear "directly connected" business purpose for the expenses incurred. A new rule on *extravagance* now applies. If legitimate travel and entertainment expenses exceed travel and per diem allowances paid to government officials, such excess may be perceived as "lavish and extravagant." If so perceived, the excess expense deduction will be disallowed. No preference is given to any particular business form.

You should not select your initial form of business on the belief that you will get more tax benefits in one form over another. For businesses started after 1986, the tax differences — if any — are truly inconsequential. Therefore, you pick your form of business based on reasons other than taxation. You may want to review again the pros and cons in Figures 2.2, 2.3, and 2.4.

Name, Logo, & Letterhead

Every new business needs a name. Select one that is intriguing, yet reasonably self-explanatory. Avoid cutesy names and those which do not convey an instant message. You want instant "name recognition": something that foretells the nature of the business you are offering.

For example, suppose you are going to start a printing business. A possible name could be "Great Impressions." But what does this convey to an ordinary person not familiar with your business. Great Impressions; so what! How about "Town & Country Printing," The "Town & Country" phrase implies that the business serves a widespread area. Or, include your own name and call it "Jones Quality Printing." Or, call it "Pony Express Printing."

The point is that you want to pick a name that is pleasant sounding, while simultaneously giving a short description of the nature of your business. To get ideas in this regard, look in the yellow pages of the phone book(s) in your area. Look up in the index your type of business, then scan the pages for competitor names. But don't try to lock horns with some competitor already in business by using a name closely resembling his.

While scanning the yellow pages, look for small advertising agencies and commercial art services. It is a good idea to contact these businesses for creative assistance. Let them help you select a name and design a logo especially for you.

A logo is a trademark or identifying symbol. It should evolve artistically from the name that you select. It may derive from one of the letters in your name, or from the initials, or by symbolizing the lead words used. For example, "Pony Express Printing" could have as its logo the initials P-E-P in some sort of a symbol, or the idea of a racing pony. Get a commercial artist enthused about your new business idea, and together you and he (or she) will come up with a name and logo that will please you.

Should you trademark register your name and logo? That all depends. Trademark registration covers names, titles, short expressions, service marks, and symbols that identify or distinguish goods and services being offered to the public. It is a good idea to register your name and logo if you expect to sell your business sometime down the road.. A TM-registered name and logo becomes a capital asset. It increases in value with time — known as "goodwill" — as the business prospers. If interested in TM registration, write to the Commissioner of Patents and Trademarks, Washington, D.C. 20231.

After settling on your name and logo, get your business stationery printed up. This includes letterheads, envelopes, business cards, customer receipts, sales invoices, fee statements, and the like. Use your name and logo in different sizes and type fonts as appropriate. While the name and logo is a capital asset (not tax deductible as an operating expense), printed stationery is an operating expense. It is fully tax deductible in the year that you commence business.

Fictitious Name Publication

You are now approaching the stage where you want to announce the availability of your business to the public. A "start-first" way to do this is to register your business name with the county clerk where your principal operations will be. Then you publish your "fictitious name" in the legal notices section in a leading newspaper in your area. It is fictitious only in the sense that your full personal name is not used.

A fictitious name publication is a sure-fire way of putting local taxing agencies and licensing authorities on notice. These agencies and authorities have staff personnel whose job is to look for these notices. When they see a new business name in print, they send out a prepackage of official application forms, rules and regulations, and threats of penalties for not contacting their offices immediately. If a particular application form applies in your case, by all means complete it and return it. If a fee is required, attach the fee. Use the minimum fee that is indicated on the fee schedule included in the prepackage.

If an application form does not fit your case, write across it in big, bold, red letters: NOT APPLICABLE. Date and sign your name, and return. If you do not do this, there will be follow-up demands, and the penalty threats will get larger and bolder.

In addition, upon publication of your fictitious name, you will receive advertising fliers from vendors, suppliers, salesmen, accountants, attorneys, consultants, and others. Save those which appeal to you, as you may need their services later.

Once in a while, your fictitious name notice will produce a "cease and desist" order by some legal firm representing an unknown competitor. Out of just pure coincidence, that competitor's name and logo may be similar to yours. If this occurs, contact the law firm for further particulars. If there is truly a close similarity, go back to your commercial artist and rename and redesign. Often, only minor changes are necessary.

There is legal purpose to your fictitious name publication. It causes you to "go on record" as to the personal name(s) of the owner(s) of the business, the official business address, and the general nature of the business intended. This means that you should select a business address which is not likely to change, even though your place of daily operations may change frequently.

Federal I.D. Number

One agency that will not respond to your fictitious name notice (there may be others) is the Internal Revenue Service (IRS). You have to contact them; they will not contact you.

Look in the front of your phone book for government agency listings. Look for the listing: Internal Revenue Service; it's there. Then look for the sublisting: Federal Tax Forms. Call that number (you may have to call it several times). Ask for **Form SS-4:** *Application for Employer Identification Number.* Ask for two or three copies in case you botch one.

In a few weeks, you'll receive Form SS-4 with instructions for completing it. It is an *application* for a federal I.D. number; it is not a tax form per se. The "SS" stands for Social Security. This means that whatever number is assigned to you will also be passed along to the Social Security Administration (SSA) for their records. As a new business employer, the SSA will be expecting you to collect social security and medicare taxes from your employees.

An edited arrangement of Form SS-4 is presented in Figure 2.5. We have edited it and rearranged it because we want to call attention to those items which are specifically addressed to new businesses.

Note in Figure 2.5 the check-boxes and blank spaces for type of organization, reason for applying, nature of business activity, to whom products and services are intended, and number of business outlets. Note also the questions about principal business location, starting date, anticipated number of employees, type of employees, and first date wages are to be paid. In the lower portion, just above your signature, you are specifically asked:

Has the applicant ever applied for an identification number for this or any other business? ☐ Yes ☐ No

Form
SS-4

APPLICATION FOR EMPLOYER IDENTIFICATION NUMBER

Name and Trade Name

Address : principal place of business

Other mailing address

Your true name
- if proprietorship

Managing partner's name
- if partnership

Principal officer's name
- if corporation

Ending month of tax year

mo ➤   yr ➤

Type
of
business

☐ Proprietorship
☐ Partnership
☐ Corporation

Nature of principal activity:
_____

Peak number of employees in next 12 months ➤

Type
of
employees

☐ Nonagricultural
☐ Agricultural
☐ Domestic

Reason
for
applying

☐ Starting new
☐ Purchased business
☐ Other _____

Principal product & raw material used:
_____

First date wages will be paid:

mo _____ day _____ yr

Starting date of business:

mo _____ day _____ yr

Selling
to
whom

☐ Businesses
☐ General public
☐ Other _____

More than one place of business?

☐ yes _____ ☐ no

Have you ever applied before? ☐ yes ☐ no
If " yes ", give particulars ➤

Signature	Date	Title	Phone No.

Fig. 2.5 - Edited Arrangement of Form SS-4

If "Yes," enter name and trade name. Also enter approx. date, city and state where the application was filed and previous number if known.

The instructions accompanying Form SS-4 tell you that every time you change the name of your business or its principal location, you have to notify the IRS. The instructions also tell you that every time you change your *form* of business — proprietorship to partnership, or partnership to corporation, or vice versa — you have to apply for a **new** tax I.D. number. Every separate business form is a tax identifying entity of its own. Don't forget this.

After processing your application, you will receive from the IRS—

NOTICE OF NEW EMPLOYER IDENTIFICATION NUMBER ASSIGNED

The number assigned will be indicated in the upper right-hand corner of the IRS notice. The text of the notice will read, in part—

The number above has been assigned to you. We will use it to identify your business tax returns and any other related documents, even if you have no employees. . . . Use the number and your name exactly as shown above on all Federal tax forms that require this information, and refer to the number in all tax payments and in tax-related correspondence or documents.

As a precautionary measure, we suggest that you file the SS-4 application approximately 60 days before you open your doors to the public. This will give you time to browse through the "Employer's Tax Guide" that the IRS will send you, plus other tax forms and instructions. This will also allow you time to set up your business bank account properly. You will have to supply to the bank your federal I.D. number.

3

BANK ACCOUNT DISCIPLINE

> Those Deposits That You Made At Your Bank(s) Are "Third-Party" Records. As Such, They Are Available For IRS Scrutiny At Any Time. Once Aware Of This, You Will Segregate Your Deposits By Tax Character, And You Will Retain The Confirmation Statements. One Day, The IRS Will Want To Compare Your Total Bank Deposits With The Total Positive Income Reported On Your Tax Return(s). All Business Expenditures, Supported With Cancelled Checks, Should Be Codified By Category And Indexed To Specific Line Numbers On Your Return(s). For Best Banking Discipline, 3-Only Accounts Are Urged (Business, Personal, And Investment).

Every new business needs capital (money). The problem is that most businesses start woefully undercapitalized. The minimum possible upfront money is advanced personally, with the expectation that the business will "bootstrap" itself on its sales. This seldom happens.

Buyers do not always pay cash. Some will take 30, 60, or 90 days to pay. The larger the buyer, the longer the delay in payment. In the meantime, you have operating expenses to pay and cost of goods to be financed. Before long, a vicious cycle of trying to borrow, fending off creditors, and delaying taxes sets in. Matters get out of control. Tax authorities step in and shut the business down.

Many of the undercapitalization problems can be avoided, we believe, by good bank accounting procedures. Indeed, disciplined bank accounting — which includes controlled access to lines of credit — is *the key* to averting the failure of any new business.

Good banking habits must start right at the beginning of your business. Don't be fooled by all of the electronic wizardry being offered by banks and financial institutions these days. Avoid those grandiose sweep accounts, electronic transfers, all-purpose investment printouts, and the mixing of personal matters with your business banking. "Putting it all on the computer" is not going to relieve you of the down-to-earth self-discipline that you need. When the chips are down, you cannot beat the old-fashioned handwritten (or typewritten) disbursement checks and the handwritten (or typewritten) deposit slips. When you get through reading this chapter, you will understand better why we say this.

Those Records at Your Bank

In case you haven't realized it, we no longer have a true free enterprise system these days. Nor do we have so-called "financial privacy." Once you are in business with a Federal I.D. Number, the IRS can monitor your banking procedures like a hawk. On short notice, it can demand that you produce the records for them, or it can gain access to your bank information without your consent. In IRS eyes, you are in business solely for the purpose of generating revenue for the U.S. Treasury.

To give you some of the flavor of what we are getting at, several years ago, a leading San Francisco newspaper ran the following advertisement—

IRS SPECIAL AGENT

Immediate opportunities exist with the IRS as special agents/criminal investigators. Duties involve <u>analyzing bank records,</u> executing search warrants, surveillance, making arrests, use of firearms and testifying in trials. [Underscoring supplied.]

"Oh, that's for crooks and tax cheats," you say. "They won't look at my bank records. I'm doing nothing wrong. Besides, they don't have the authority to go to my bank, without my consent. That's invasion of privacy!"

Well, well.

Be introduced, now, to the following six sections of the Internal Revenue Code:

Sec. 7601 — Canvassing for Taxable Persons and Objects

Sec. 7602 — Examination of Books and Witnesses

Sec. 7603 — Service of Summons

Sec. 7604 — Enforcement of Summons

Sec. 7605 — Time and Place of Examination

Sec. 7606 — Entry of Premises for Examination of Taxable Objects

The term "taxable objects" means . . . *any books, papers, records, or other data which may be relevant or material.* Thus, the combined effect of these six sections is that the IRS can get to your bank records whenever it wants to. In theory, there must be some pretense that tax is due. In practice, a $1 allegation provides sufficient cause. The IRS can go to your bank in the daytime, or at night, if it is open then.

In Section 7609(a): *Special Procedures for Third-Party Summons*, your bank is defined as a *third-party recordkeeper*. As such, your bank records AT THE BANK belong to the bank: not to you. True, it is your business financial information that goes to the bank. But that's not the point. The records are "third-party." This means that the IRS need give your bank only three days' notice. After that, the bank has to produce its records on you, whether you consent or not.

Please do not misunderstand. We're not trying to put the fear of God in you. We just want you to face reality. We don't want you to be blind and blithe about your banking procedures. If you are truly aware that your financial transactions — especially when in business — are an "open book" for the IRS at any time, you'll take prompt action to avoid surprises.

Ordinarily, the IRS will not go to your bank (or other financial institution) on its own whim. Except in rare criminal investigatory cases, it first seeks your bank records from you. A "bank," incidentally, is a *depository* institution through which financial transactions are processed in the normal course of business. Therefore, what the IRS is primarily interested in is the TOTAL DEPOSITS that you made, and how this total reconciles with the income reported on your business tax returns.

A Nightmarish Example

Not long ago, a small business owner (let's call him Big Foot Instrument Co.) received a "routine" form letter from the IRS. In those parts pertinent to our discussion, it read—

Your return for the above year has been selected for examination. Please provide the following:
- *All records and books to determine income (deposit slips, check registers, cash receipts, sales journals, books of account, account numbers, . . . and any other records used to determine income).*
- *All records, contracts, statements, and any other documentation of nontaxable income.*
- *Monthly statements for all financial accounts, both business and personal.*

If you were to receive a similar IRS demand, what would *you* do? Could you pull together in one place "all records of income"?

The gross sales and other income from the Big Foot business totaled $294,000 . . . as reported on his tax return.

In the case at hand, there were five different financial accounts. All were handled by the same bank. The types of accounts and the total deposits in each were as follows:

1.	The business account	$224,000
2.	Line-of-credit account	115,000
3.	Personal checking account	327,000
4.	Rental collection account	32,000
5.	Personal investment account	138,000
	Grand total deposits	$836,000

Big Foot reported $294,000 on his tax return. What accounts for the difference of $542,000 (836,000 minus 294,000)? Is it income not reported? If so, it is fully taxable . . . plus penalties . . . plus interest.

Now you must surely feel the anguish and nightmares that owner Big Foot went through. To make matters worse, he destroyed all of his deposit slips and his investment redemption statements. He did "everything by computer." He engaged profusely in telephone transfers between accounts. His line-of-credit was automatically re-extended when his loan balance was paid down below $100,000. Since all of his accounts were with the same bank, all monthly statements looked alike, except for the 15-digit account numbers.

In Big Foot's own heart, he knew that all of his taxable income was properly reported. But how would he prove this to a skeptical government agent whose grand promotion is riding on the additional revenue from a $542,000 "discrepancy"?

This is a perfect example of what careless banking habits can do. It's all so easy with a telephone and a computer. The IRS simply will not accept your computer printouts. Thus, until you have been through the bank-deposits-analysis-wringer by a tax agent drooling for more revenue, you cannot imagine the pain and suffering that lie in wait. If your business grosses more than $100,000, then you, too, are vulnerable.

How It All Worked Out

In the example above, the $32,000 rental collection account was not Big Foot's own money. A close business friend who owned several apartment complexes went on a foreign vacation for three months. He asked Big Foot to be his collection agent while he was gone. Of course, there was no contract; no written agreement; just a verbal understanding. To keep the rent money separate, Big Foot opened a separate account in his own name, with his own bank. Most of the money was used to pay operating expenses. When the friend returned, the balance in the rental account was turned over to him. It took a long, hard time to prove this to the tax agent. It was not until the agent examined the friend's bank account that he allowed the $32,000 as an offset against Big Foot's $542,000 discrepancy. The reduced discrepancy now stood at $510,000.

Next came the $115,000 line-of-credit account. These were not actual deposits but were repayments on a cumulative $215,000 loan which the bank had advanced to Big Foot. The repayments came from Big Foot's other three accounts (business, personal, and investment). But every repayment (about 15 in all) had to be individually traced. This necessitated showing 15 origins in the three accounts and tracing each one through, telephone transfer by telephone transfer. In the process, approximately 56 monthly statements had to be reviewed. In time, Big Foot prevailed. The tax agent allowed a $115,000 offset against the $510,000 discrepancy. The revised discrepancy now stood at $395,000 — still a long way to go.

The next matter was: Where did the $215,000 line-of-credit loans go? Big Foot contacted his bank to help him establish the amount and date that each loan originated. He repeatedly asked for a computer printout summary. The bank fouled this up miserably due to its interoffice retrieval problems and due to the fact that the bank's central loan office was some 1,000 miles away. Finally, though, he got the summary showing that eight loans were advanced to him. Big Foot then had to trace through to show where each of the loans went into which of his three accounts (business, personal, and investment). Ultimately, he did so, even though by this time he was a nervous wreck. Begrudgingly, the tax agent allowed another offset of $215,000 against the $395,000 discrepancy. This third-time revised discrepancy now stood at $180,000.

Big Foot recalled that several of his T-bills matured that year, and that he had redeemed some mutual fund shares. He wasn't sure of the total amount, but thought is was around $150,000. The problem was he didn't have his confirmation statements. Nor was he sure into which of his three accounts (business, personal, or investment) the money was deposited. After contacting and recontacting his brokerage firm, he got duplicate confirmation that three T-bills matured for $120,000 and that two mutual fund redemptions amounted to $27,269. Because they were in even amounts, he was able to trace the T-bill deposits rather easily. Being odd-figure amounts, the two mutual fund deposits were more difficult. In fact, he never did find any exact match. However, he found two deposit amounts which were within a few hundred dollars of the two redemption checks. Seeing that Big Foot was really trying, the tax agent allowed $147,000 offset against the $180,000 discrepancy. The residual discrepancy was now down to $33,000.

Suddenly, Big Foot remembered that he loaned his brother $25,000 several years ago. There was no written promissory payback note to this effect. But his wife remembered depositing the $25,000 payback in their personal checking account. This deposit was easily identified . . . BUT. How could the tax agent be sure that the $25,000 wasn't "skim money" that Big Foot took from his business? The brother had to be called in. He was asked to make a written declaration "under penalties of perjury" that he indeed borrowed $25,000 from Big Foot. The brother also had to produce his own financial records showing where and when he deposited the money. In a sense of desperation, the tax agent allowed the $25,000 offset against the $33,000 discrepancy. He said, however, "This is it. No more. You have taken six weeks of my time and my supervisor is pressing me to close the case."

At this point, Big Foot, too, was weary. The unexplained discrepancy was now down to $8,000. (This was less than 3% of his $294,000 reported income.) Reluctantly, he consented to the $8,000 being tax treated as an "income deficiency." This meant that he would have to pay additional tax. Better on $8,000 than on $542,000!

Throughout the six-week ordeal, Big Foot never slept soundly. Many a night he woke up in a cold sweat trying to recall his various deposit transactions. "It was a hellish nightmare," he said. "I'll never go through that again. I've learned my lesson."

How to Start Right

Big Foot, like so many other entrepreneurs who became successful, never took seriously the stories he heard of others who had their bank deposits tax examined. His conscience was clear . . . but not his depository trails.

So, what are the lessons that Big Foot learned? There are five, namely—

First. When in business, have only one business account and do not involve it with other accounts that you may control. Keep the business account in a separate depository institution from all others. You want it so isolated that every deposit to it can be separately traced.

Second. The number of depository accounts under your control should be no more than three at any one time. These should be:
(1) a business account (checking only)
(2) a personal account (checking/savings)
(3) an investment account (checking/savings)
Preferably, each account should be in a separate depository institution of its own. This is to avoid similarity of monthly statements and practices. This is also to avoid the compounding of computer and interoffice foulups by an "all-accounts-in-one" establishment.

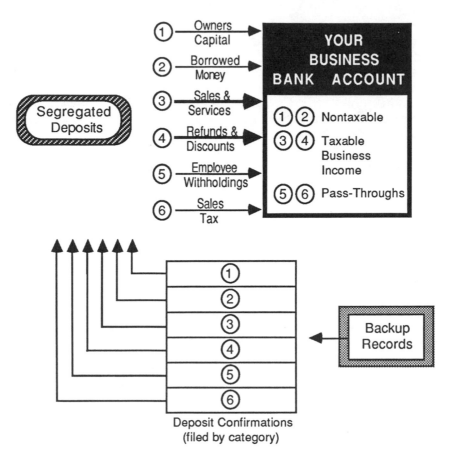

Fig. 3.1 - Character of Deposits Into Business Bank Account

A "depository account" is one in which you place money with the expectation of withdrawing and disbursing that money frequently throughout the year. This includes trading and rollover accounts. Long-term investments and long-term loans are not depository in nature.

Third. Identify every deposit or group of deposits by its *tax character*. Make separate deposits for each separate tax character. Obtain — and keep — the deposit confirmations; mark on your copy the tax character of each. We list in Figure 3.1 the tax character of those deposits most likely to occur in a small business. Your experience may uncover others. Avoid being a collection agent or check casher for other people's money.

Fourth. At the deposit entries on every monthly bank statement, make a notation cross-referencing them to the deposit confirmation documents that you have. Index and file the deposit confirmations in a separate system, along the lines indicated in Figure 3.1. You want immediate access to those confirmations when the tax attack comes.

Fifth. At the end of each tax year, tally the total deposits in all (three) of your bank accounts. Compare this with the total positive income reported on your personal and business tax returns. Reconcile any discrepancy promptly. Don't wait until several years after the fact, when the IRS comes on the scene.

Why do we say 3-only depository accounts? Because the human mind associates more readily with distinctions between three items than between five, seven, or other number.

Our depiction of a 3-only banking scheme is presented in Figure 3.2. Note that each account is in a separate financial institution of its own. This forces you to consciously make a decision — and make a paper trail — when you transfer money between accounts.

"Big Stub" Business Checks

The IRS tax letter to Big Foot (in our nightmarish example above) also included the following demand:

All records and books to determine deductions, expenses, tax credits, and prepayment credits: invoices, cancelled checks, cash receipts, contracts, escrows, statements, diary, calendar, travel logs, policies for insurance, tax bills, inventory records, worksheets, and any other records used to determine deductions and expenses.

For our purposes at the moment, the key item in the above paragraph that we want to focus on is *cancelled checks*. When you are in business, and you disburse money from your business bank account, your cancelled checks are unsurpassed for establishing "proof of payment." This is because they are third-party

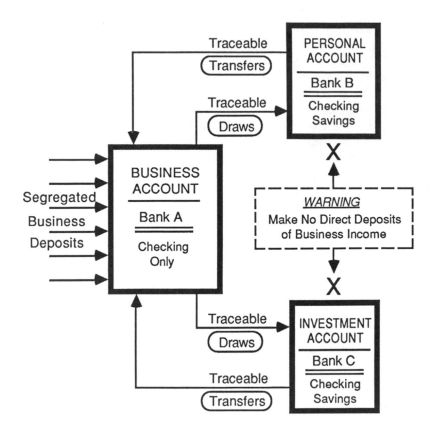

Fig. 3.2 - Banking Discipline With 3-Only Accounts

documents. They have been processed through the banking system in a manner over which you had no control. Cancelled checks are prima facie evidence of transactional facts. You want these cancelled checks in your permanent records.

Good cancelled-check practices require that your business checks be large in size: both the check and its stub. We call these "big stub" checks. You want enough space and lines to write (or type) descriptive notes and cross references. Ideally, you want the check and its stub to be self-explanatory when you have to tax-hunt for it three to five years down the road.

Commercial banks and accounting-form designers have all sorts of check-writing recordkeeping schemes. We suggest that you examine several, and select the scheme that best fits your particular business. But don't get too fancy. You don't want to be a slave to accounting mechanics. All you want is to be able to identify, by cross-referencing to other documents, every disbursement check that you write. Prenumbered checks and prenumbered stubs are very helpful in this regard.

The ideal scheme, we think, consists of three essential elements. These elements are:

1. A coding/indexing system that correlates with the itemized expenditures on your business tax return.
2. A means (big stubs, full ledgers, check journals) for systematically recording each prenumbered check as it is written, with a code/index number hand-entered thereon.
3. A sequential easy-to-retrieve hard copy file of the cancelled checks, as they are returned from the bank.

Since this is not an accounting book (it is a "tax guide"), we want to stress the protective elements involved but not the particulars. Towards this end, we present Figure 3.3. Note that in the codifying index — and on the cancelled checks themselves — we are trying to key into *every line entry* on your business tax schedules. If you make this tie-in as you go along, you'll have sleepful nights when the tax wolf growls.

How you keep your personal checking and investment/savings accounts is up to you. Just be sure that you do *not* pay any business expenditures from those accounts. If you advance money to, or transfer it from, your business account, do so in even-dollar increments (in $100 or $1,000 amounts) . . . with clear paper trails.

Cash and Barter?

There is one subject on which little is written, but which is on every tax agent's mind. All that green-cash you received in your business; what did you do with it? How do you account for it? And what about all that bartering you do? Do you report it?

Some tax agents have fanciful imaginations about bundles of cash coming in which you are skimming off. Without specific facts, they can't directly accuse you of this. But they are thinking about it all the time: cash and barter. They deftly try to catch you off guard, then pounce on you.

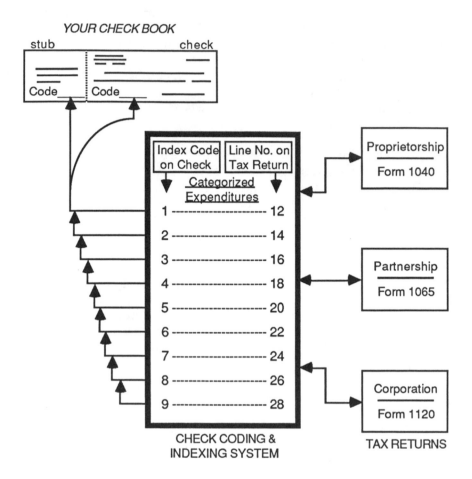

Fig. 3.3 - Coding/Indexing of Business Expenses to Tax Returns

In many businesses, there just aren't significant opportunities for cash transactions and barter. Take a medical or dental office, for example. Most patients let their insurance plans pay the bill, or they pay by check and seek insurance reimbursement for themselves. In other professional practices, clients want receipts, not for insurance purposes, but possibly for tax deduction purposes. In mail-order businesses, how many customers would dare send cash in the mail? In any of these examples, the opportunity for cash and bartering is minimal.

On the other hand, some businesses are quite susceptible. For example, restaurants, neighborhood retail stores, beauty salons, handyman shops, repair services, landscape maintenance, independent contractors, and the like are vulnerable. In these businesses, cash is king and barter is queen. Some probably are part of the underground economy.

If you are in a "suspected business" where cash and bartering are common, you must prepare a *cash journal*. Whether you enter every 10-cent transaction or not is your affair. But you'd better make some entries. Enter the date, amount, name of person, and purpose of the transaction. Enter the cash received, cash paid out, barter value received, and barter value given. A cash journal, more or less kept up to date, is generally accepted as evidence of your good faith in trying to accurately record your business income.

Here's our rule-of-thumb on the keeping of cash journals. If your cash and bartering transactions are truly less than 5% of your otherwise gross sales and/or receipts for the year, forget about a cash journal. If you were to prepare one in which your cash and barter receipts turned out to be, say, 3%, a tax agent would suspect that you were not keeping a full and correct record.

On the other hand, if your cash and barter receipts do reach 5% or more of your gross for the year, we strongly advise you to keep such a journal. If you do not, the IRS will impute to you an unreported cash amount based on its statistical studies of businesses of your type. Without a cash journal, you are in no position to dispute the IRS.

The "De Minimis" Rule

Why are we so confident of our 5% no-cash-journal threshold? Because of the *de minimis rule* in the tax code. This rule appears not too clearly in Section 132(e) (employee fringe benefits) and in Section 280A(g) (certain rental use). In tax jargon, the term "de minimis" means—

Any property or service the value of which is . . . so small as to make accounting for it unreasonable or administratively impracticable. [Sec. 132(e)(1)]

We can find no actual percentage figure in the tax code. However, Section 280A(g) uses the phrase—

less than 15 days during the taxable year . . . shall not be included in the gross income.

This excerpt relates to the de minimis rental of one's personal residence. The resulting fraction is 15/365 which is 4.11% (exactly). Hence, we are interpreting "less than 5%" as constituting de minimis.

Whether de minimis or not, all cash received in a business is supposed to be tax reported. How do you do this if no cash journal is maintained? You simply deposit it in your business bank account.

Every bank has its deposit slips designed to accommodate cash amounts. There is a CASH line on the deposit form. This line is sub-lined into two parts: currency and coin. If, throughout the year, you had at least a few of your (confirmed) deposit slips with cash entries, you have third-party documentation in your favor. It would be difficult then for an overzealous tax agent to assert his (or her) wild guess as to what your cash receipts might have been.

If you are in a business which uses a cash register and accepts credit cards, you are probably above cash-and-barter suspicion. This is because electronic cash registers are automatic cash-flow computers. Daily, weekly, and monthly tapes are printed out which are difficult to tamper with. The same applies to credit cards. They, too, are virtually tamper proof by the business owner. Cash registers and credit cards, therefore, are approved substitutes for cash journals.

Borrowed Money

Most every business, particularly when starting new, needs to borrow money to keep its operation going. Borrowed money is *not* taxable income. The concern, however, is that the borrowed money is added to and commingled with taxable income of the business. This causes the depository tracing problem that we discussed earlier. Unless a borrowed deposit is positively traceable to its lending source, you can wind up paying income tax on your borrowed money.

There are two classes of borrowed money: commercial and noncommercial. Commercial lenders are banks and financial institutions; noncommercial lenders are family and friends. In a sense, owner's capital also is a form of borrowed money. But it has the element of risk which lender money does not have.

New businesses tend to be lax in keeping all forms of borrowed money separately identified. Our position is that *every act of borrowing* (including owner capital) should be separately documented. In this regard, automatic lines of credit can be a disservice. Automatic credit is a blending of rollovers of one loan into another, then into another . . . and so on. We suggest some system of "controlled access" to this credit. You want to know exactly when each advance is made, and how much. Line-of-credit running accounts often are difficult to decipher when a deposits-tracing tax agent is breathing down your neck.

Tracing the origin of noncommercial loans can be a real bear. Often, family and friends write out a check and turn it over to the borrower. He then deposits it in his business account. Because of mutual trust, neither takes the time to prepare any documentation on the terms of their agreement. Seldom is any straight-forward promissory note ever written.

Promissory notes are so common that preprinted forms are available in the legal forms section of office supply stores. These preprinted forms contain all of the "promise to pay" legal wording. They also contain blank spaces for entering the amount of principal borrowed, the terms of repayment, rate of interest, due date, and name(s) of the borrower(s). Promissory notes do not have to be notarized, but they can be. Any one in business should have a pad of promissory notes among his stationery supplies. When a non-commercial loan is consummated with your handshake, whip out a blank promissory note and fill it in. This is an easy way to document the act. It can save you many tax headaches later.

Employee Withholdings & Sales Tax

When you go into business, are you aware that you automatically become a tax collector? You will not get paid for the job. You will not even get a courtesy "thanks." You will have all of the displeasures of enforcing collection and all of the burdens for accounting for the monies collected. It is a thankless job.

There are two categories of tax collections forced upon you. If you have employees, you must withhold certain amounts from the compensation you pay them. (We will devote an entire chapter to this matter, namely: Chapter 4.) If you sell or service retail, you must collect sales tax. (We'll devote Chapter 5 to this matter.) None of these withholdings and collections are your money. Nor are they monies generated by the business itself. These items are *other people's tax money* (OPTM) which passes through your hands.

What do you do with this money? Do you deposit it in your business account? Or, do you deposit it in a separate account?

Whatever you do, you had better know what the amount is at all times. You should have separate columnar entries in whatever books of account that you keep. Your bookkeeping scheme should be such that you can ascertain — to the day and minute — the cumulative total of such money collected.

In your book entries on the cumulative totals, you should make some kind of highlighted notation such as: OPTM (other people's tax money). Call this your "NEVER TOUCH" money. If you never touch this money, it will be readily available for turning over to the respective tax agencies when it is due. Many a small business errs badly on this matter.

What happens, usually, is that the OPTM is routinely deposited in the business bank account. It is mixed in with ordinary business income with no separate depository distinction. This inflates the cash balance on hand. Unthinkingly, it is made available for other expenditures for the business. When the statutory clock comes due for turning the OPTM over to the proper tax agencies, the OPTM is not there. New money has to be borrowed for taxes. Thus, unconsciously, the vicious money-cycle commences for getting further and further behind.

Depending on the magnitude of OPTM collected, some businesses open a separate tax account. This is not a bad idea, particularly if the OPTM exceeds 20% of your other business income. If you do open a separate account, you might also add your employer tax money (which is different from employee withholdings) and any excise tax money (which is different from sales tax). An entirely separate bank account exclusively for tax deposits can help to avoid dipping into that money for ordinary business expenditures.

Whether you deposit the OPTM into your regular business account, or open a separate account, we have no preference. Much depends on your own self-discipline and your ability to separate — at least in your mind — the different types of money that you are handling. If you can do this, and keep record books accordingly, there is much convenience and simplicity in having one-only business account.

4

EMPLOYER TAX MATTERS

One Publication You "Must Have" Is IRS CIRCULAR E (Employer's Tax Guide). It Gives Tables And Instructions For Income Tax And Social Security Withholdings. Every Employee Increases Your Tax Paperwork For Such Items As Form SS-5 (Social Security Number), Form W-4 (Withholding Allowances), Form 940 (Unemployment Tax), Form 941 (Quarterly Returns), Form 8109 (Tax Deposits) And — Of Course — Form W-2 (Wage And Tax Statement). Interpretive Care Is Required On Taxability Of Reported Tips, Fringe Benefits, And Expense Allowances. A Written Employment Agreement, A Separate File — And Separate Payroll Ledger — On Each Employee Are Essential.

If you hire one employee, 100 employees, or 1,000 employees, your tax paperwork is the same. Instead of concentrating on trying to make your business prosper, you are forced into being a tax collector. You have to withhold money from your employees, add some of your own, and turn it over to federal and state agencies. This is truly an imposition. You get no appreciation whatsoever from the government agencies whose work you do.

There are only two ways to avoid this imposition. One way is to be totally self-employed and have no employees at all. The second way is to engage only independent contractors. Neither of these two alternatives is practical, if you want your business to sustain gross sales in excess of $100,000 while reaching for $1,000,000 or more. So, at some point, you will have to face the tax reality of employees.

There is irony in your predicament. Not only do you have to impose on your employees government's will — and fence their complaints — you are actually taxed for the privilege of employing them. This is the "employer tax" aspect of doing business. The taxes on you as an employer are: (a) social security tax, (b) medicare tax, (c) federal unemployment tax, (d) state unemployment tax, and (e) state training tax (in some states). Also in the works are new federal mandates. Thus, when you hire employees, you are taxed on the possibility of their becoming sick or unemployed and for the day when they retire. These employer taxes are irrespective of any retirement plans and fringe benefits that you might otherwise adopt for your employees.

IRS Circular E

When your application for a federal I.D. number is processed, you are added automatically to IRS's Employer Notification Program. That is, unless you instruct them otherwise, they will send you applicable publications, posters, instructions, directives, tax forms, and on and on. Among the mailings is IRS Circular E: **Employer's Tax Guide.** If you do not receive one within 30 days after being assigned an employer I.D., we urge you to phone the IRS and obtain one. Call the listed number which says: "Tax Forms Only." Circular E is a tax form. We suppose the "E" is for employer-employee.

Circular E consists of 60+ pages of 2-columnar text and tables. On the first inside page, it gives you a tax calendar and due date for completing all of the employer-employee forms you have to file. You are told explicitly that—

This guide tells you about your tax responsibilities as an employer. It explains the requirements for withholding, depositing, reporting, and paying taxes. It explains the forms you must give your employees, those your employees must give you, and those you must send to the IRS and SSA [Social Security Administration]. . . . This guide also has tax tables you need to figure the taxes to withhold for each employee.

Circular E also tells you who your employees are. This is a broad directive which says that—

Anyone who performs services is an employee if you, as an employer, can control what will be done and how it will be done. This is so even when you give the employee freedom of action. What matters is that you have the legal right to control the method and result of the services. . . . The employer usually gives the worker the tools and place to work and has the right to fire the worker.

Circular E is updated every year in January. Every employer should have the latest Circular E in his reference library on tax matters. This is a "must."

In a manner similar to the IRS, state employment-tax agencies also issue their version of Employer's Tax Guide and Withholding Tables. These state agencies have their own tax calendar and tax forms which you must complete. Thus, not only do you have responsibility to Big Brother, you have responsibility to his Little Brother, too.

What If Nonemployees?

As you might suspect, Circular E does not tell you how to qualify some persons as nonemployees. If you had nonemployees, you would escape the withholding and tax reporting responsibilities. Circular E tries to discourage you from even thinking in these terms.

In a taunting manner, Circular E says—

If an employer-employee relationship exists, it does not matter what it is called. The employee may be called a partner, agent, or independent contractor. It also does not matter how payments are measured or paid, what they are called, or whether the employee works full- or part-time.

The Circular does go on to say that—

If you have good reason for treating a worker other than as an employee, you will not be liable for employment taxes on the payments to that worker.

This raises the obvious question: What constitutes "good reason" for treating a worker other than an employee? Circular E avoids discussing this issue altogether. However, this question is addressed in a separate pronouncement of its own: Information

Release No. 87-8. This pronouncement cites 20 — yes, 20 — IRS tests that a person must pass in order to have good reason to believe that he/she is not an employee. We summarize these 20 tests for you in Figure 4.1. As you can see, it is very difficult to claim that a worker is a nonemployee.

Information Release 87-8 (summarized in Figure 4.1) was specifically designed to thwart the treatment of certain skilled workers as nonemployees. Engineers, designers, drafters, computer programmers, system analysts, and similar persons must be treated as employees if they work at your place of business — or are under your direction — on a substantially full-time basis. If you treat these persons as nonemployees, *you* are directly liable for their income tax and social security tax withholdings. If you want a decision as to whether a worker is an employee or nonemployee, file **Form SS-8** with the IRS.

In other parts of Circular E, the IRS has imposed its will on traditionally recognized nonemployees. This includes route salesmen, insurance agents, traveling salesmen, and homeworkers using employer-provided materials and instructions. Even though for income tax purposes, these persons may be treated as nonemployees, for social security tax purposes they must be treated as employees. This means that you have to withhold their portion of the social security tax and contribute an equal portion from your own business.

When Hiring Any Employee

Certain tax information must be obtained from every employee when first hired, and supplying it should be a condition of his or her employment. The two most important items in this regard are social security number and Form W-4 (withholding allowances). As simple as it may sound, it is surprising the number of small businesses that hire employees without first getting this information nailed down.

Consider, for example, the social security number. Some potential hirees can't remember their number or they transpose the digits. There are nine digits in that number. The whole world of taxation and tax reporting is keyed to this number. If it is ever incorrectly reported on a tax form, it takes months and years to straighten the matter out. Allow no hiree, therefore, to say that he will provide it to you "later." You want it now, or no hire-on.

FACTORS INDICATIVE OF EMPLOYEE STATUS

1. Instructions
   - as to when, where, & how
2. Training
   - under supervision of others
3. Integration
   - directly into daily operations
4. Personal services
   - using own skills & talents
5. Hiring & firing
   - subject to : by employer
6. Continuity
   - daily ongoing relationship
7. Hours of work
   - when / where set & fixed

8. Time devoted
   - as substantially full time
9. Work on premises
   - not permitted elsewhere
10. Sequences set
    - nil deviations allowed
11. Reports required
    - either oral or written
12. Paid regularly
    - by hour, week, or month
13. Reimbursement
    - for business & travel expense
14. Tools & materials
    - primarily by employer

FACTORS INDICATIVE OF NONEMPLOYEE STATUS

15. Significant investment
    - in facilities (such as office and/or shop) and in major equipment.

16. Realization of profit or loss
    - accepting the risks of work performed in a competitive environment.

17. More than one customer
    - services for a multiple of unrelated persons or firms at the same time.

18. Available to general public
    - continuous offering of services without expectation of long-term hire.

19. "Contract" services
    - written or oral, where results are specified but not manner of performance.

20. Incurring of liability
    - if results are unsatisfactory, subject to lawsuit and rework.

Fig. 4.1 - Factors for Determining Employee/Nonemployee Status

As an employer, your best protection is to insist on seeing the hiree's **Social Security Number Card.** This is that wallet-size little card issued by the Social Security Administration (SSA). This card displays the social security number in bold red figures, followed by the typed full name of the person and his/her handwritten signature. We strongly urge you to *photocopy* this card. Then attach the photocopy to the record on that employee.

If a hiree does not have a social security card, insist that he obtain one. It is not your concern why he does not have one; it is your concern that he have one. For this purpose, instruct the hiree to fill out **Form SS-5**: Application for a Social Security Number Card (Original, Replacement, or Correction). It is a good idea for you to have a stack of SS-5 forms on hand at all times. Get them from the IRS or SSA. You also should know the address of the nearest Social Security office to your place of business. A lot of hire-on time can be saved, with accurate knowledge on how to get a social security card.

The next matter, before taking on an employee, is Form W-4. This form is officially titled: *Employee's Withholding Allowance Certificate.* Note that this is *not* an "exemption" certificate; it is a "withholding allowance" certificate. You also should have a stack of these forms on hand at all times.

Before you take any withholding from an employee's pay, you want to have an *originally signed* Form W-4 in your possession. This form provides the employee's full name, current address, and his marital status. If an employee delays in providing you with his W-4, treat him as a single person with one allowance only. Do not try to guess and do your employee a favor. If it turns out later that he has to pay additional income taxes (beyond the withholdings) he is going to blame you.

Do not fall into the trap of trying to help an employee to fill out his W-4. The best you can offer is to obtain his true marital status, and the true number of dependents that he is supporting. Beyond that, instruct him to go to the nearest IRS office for help or to a tax preparer of his choice. The W-4 form is not the model of simplicity and clearness that one would like. Technically, you should request a new W-4 from each employee at the beginning of each year.

If an employee claims more than 10 withholding allowances on his W-4, you are required to send his form to the IRS. If so required, send the original form (showing the employee's own signature), but keep a photocopy in your records on the employee. Subsequently, the IRS will computer-slap a $500 penalty on the employee. This will spur him to complete a detailed questionnaire and computation sheet to justify the proper number of allowances.

When an employee gets an IRS notice of the $500 W-4 penalty, chances are he will come running back to you. To anticipate this, it is good practice to notify the employee in writing when you are forwarding his W-4 to the IRS. You might also suggest that he be prepared to fill out a lengthy justification questionnaire. You might also afford him the opportunity to reconsider the W-4 that he provided to you.

Separate Record on Each Employee

In some businesses, employer-employee tax problems can be irritating. The problems can haunt you up to as much as five years after termination of an employee. In addition, there can be labor and legal problems: disputes over pay, reimbursement for expenses, fringe benefits, and so on. It is important, therefore, that you keep an entirely separate record on each employee. Do not try to shortcut and combine several employee records for your own convenience.

In the record file of each hire-on, you should have an *Employment Agreement*. This should be one or two pages of particulars. It should be read and signed by the hire-on, and should be countersigned by you or a member of your staff. The amount of compensation should be indicated, together with the hours of work expected, some standard of performance, designation of the work place (or sales territory), and the furnishing of tools, vehicles, and incidental materials. A statement of your policy on expense reimbursement, fringe benefits, and retirement plans (if any) should be included. We discourage the setup of pension and profit-sharing plans until you have been in business for at least three years. If you have no such plans, you should state so in the employment agreement. This way, an employee may be eligible to set up his own IRA plan. (IRA = Individual Retirement Account.)

If you have to terminate an employee for any reason, you must prepare for the file a memorandum of the circumstances therewith. Terminated employees may find it necessary to apply for unemployment benefits. Each application for said benefits will be followed by an inquiry to you. On state official forms, you will be asked to verify the termination, the cause, and length of service of the employee. Unless you keep a written record on each employee, you may have to grope and guess.

One of the common problems in a small business is the rapid turnover of employees. Often, they are young persons trying to test their own interests. Because of this turnover, a *probation period* is recommended. To save tax paperwork during the probation, it is advisable to contract with a temporary service agency to supply the workers you need. This way, the temporary service agency becomes the employer who has to keep the tax and other records. A temporary service contract of from three to six months should be adequate to determine whether you want to take on a worker as a regular employee.

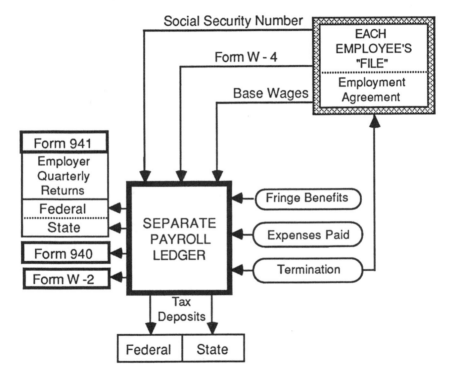

Fig. 4.2 - Typical Records Needed on Each Employee

As an indication of the amount of paperwork required on each employee, we present Figure 4.2. Note that the central tax document is a payroll ledger. This ledger and the other items portrayed are discussed below. The intended message in Figure 4.2

is that when you take on any employee, your tax duties are increased substantially.

Payroll Ledgers: Setup & Selection

On the very day that a new employee starts, you should set up a payroll ledger in his or her behalf. Do not wait until the first payday arrives. Formulate the payroll ledger the moment an employee reports aboard. Obtain and record his full name, current address, social security number, marital status, and the W-4 withholding allowances. There should be a separate ledger for each employee. The obvious reason for this is that each employee will have payroll particulars of his own.

Be sure that each employee understands the "payroll period" involved. This is the period for which the *base pay* is computed. It may be weekly, biweekly (every two weeks), semimonthly (twice a month), or monthly. Other periods may be used, but these are the most common. Separate tax withholding tables are based on each of these periods (in Circular E).

Payroll ledgers are designed in columnar form. The first column is used to record the base pay for the period covered. In addition to base pay, there may be supplemental pay such as prizes and awards, bonuses, commissions, sick pay, and so on. Included in the "and so on" are taxable fringe benefits. All of this *other pay* should be grouped together in a separate column of its own. There should be itemized notations indicating the breakdown, if more than one type of other pay is involved.

In some businesses, tips become an important element in an employee's gross pay. If an employee receives tips of $20 or more in a month, he is supposed to report the total amount to you. These become known as *taxable tips* which you include on his payroll ledger. In food and beverage establishments, *allocated tips* (also taxable) are assigned to each employee whether he/she reports them to you or not. A separate column on the ledger should be made available for all tip inclusions.

A *gross pay* column should be provided to tally all of the separate forms of compensation due each employee. This includes the taxable fringes and taxable tips. It is from the gross pay that the income tax withholdings apply. There are federal income tax withholdings and state/local income tax withholdings (where applicable).

There also should be a separate column for social security and medicare taxable amounts. The social security taxable base can — and often does — differ from the gross pay amount. Certain fringes and other forms of compensation are not social security taxable, though they are fully income taxable. Distinguishing between the different tax bases can be troublesome in some cases.

Altogether, there are from four to six separate *required withholdings* from the compensation due each employee. The variation depends on state and local tax laws, and on whether any taxable tips are reported to you. The required withholdings are—

1. Federal income tax (FIT)
2. Social security tax (SST)
3. Medicare tax (MCT)
4. State income tax (SIT)
   (except for those few states which have no income tax)
5. State disability insurance (SDI)
6. Local income tax (LIT)
   (for those few cities, regions, and counties that require it)

In addition to the required withholdings, there may be voluntary withholdings. These could be savings plans, group health payments, and loan repayments. There may also be involuntary withholdings. There could be court-ordered child and/or spousal support payments, tax liens for prior delinquencies, and other judgment liens. As an employer, you are responsible for these withholdings also.

What does all the above mean?

It means that there is no universal format of payroll ledger to serve all business needs. Each business has to select a ledger format that fulfills its employee pay practices. A variety of preprinted ledger forms can be found in most office supply and stationery stores. You should pick and choose among those formats which are nearly self-explanatory for your particular needs. In all cases, however, make sure that the ledgers are formatted into four separate calendar quarters for the year.

Employer Quarterly Returns

There is one matter that you cannot simplify, minimize, or avoid. If you have one employee and withhold so much as $1 from that employee, you become locked in to a quarterly tax reporting system. In the federal domain you are required to file Form 941: *Employer's Quarterly Federal Tax Return.* Similarly, states also have their version of quarterly employer returns.

The term "quarterly" means every three months . . . without fail. These are calendar quarters, as follows:

Quarter	Ending	Due Date
Jan - Feb - Mar	Mar. 31	Apr. 30
Apr - May - Jun	Jun. 30	Jul. 31
Jul - Aug - Sep	Sep. 30	Oct. 31
Oct - Nov - Dec	Dec. 31	Jan. 31

As you can see, the due date of these returns is 30 days after the end of each quarter. For each whole or part month that a return is filed late, there is a 5% penalty. The penalty is paid by the employer: *not* by the employees. This is what we mean by being "locked in" to the system.

To introduce you to Form 941, we present a simplified and edited version of it in Figure 4.3. We have generalized the form so that you will understand its purpose, without bogging you down with preparatory details. Whether you complete the form yourself, or have a payroll service agency do it for you, is another matter. However prepared, you would be the one to sign it. As the business owner, therefore, you should be fully aware of all employee tax matters.

In Figure 4.3, we have emphasized certain key lines that you should know about. The first line of importance is "Wages, tips, and other compensation" paid during the quarter (line 1). This is the gross amount against which employee income taxes are withheld. These withholdings appear on lines 2 through 4 (in Fig. 4.3). These withholdings are *not* your money. Other than your time and effort, you contribute nothing towards these withholdings. They are 100% employees' money.

Lines 5 through 8 (in Fig. 4.3) are social security and medicare tax matters. The spaces are for entering the amount of wages, tips, and other compensation to which the social security and medicare taxes apply. In some cases, this is not the same as the amount on line 1. This is because certain kinds of employees and certain kinds of payments are not subject to the social security/medicare tax. To determine whether or not a certain amount is exempt from social security/medicare tax, we refer you to Circular E. Look for the table

Form 941	EMPLOYER'S QUARTERLY FEDERAL TAX RETURN	
Name (of owner) _____ Trade Name _____ Address_____ _____	Quarter Ending	☐ Mar 31 ☐ Jun 30 ☐ Sep 30 ☐ Dec 31
	Employer I.D.No. _____	

1.	Total Wages, Tips, & Other Compensation		$
2.	Total income tax withheld		
3.	Adjustments (if any): Explain		
4.	Adj. total income tax withheld		
5.	Social security wages & tips	X 12.4 %	
6.	Medicare wages & tips	X 2.9 %	
7.	Adjustments (if any): Explain		
8.	Adj. total social security & medicare tax		
9.	Total taxes (add lines 4 and 8)		
10.	Total deposits for quarter		
	BALANCE DUE (subtract line 10 from 9)		
	(should be less than $500) PAY TO IRS		

RECORD OF DEPOSITS (Form 8109): Complete if line 9 is $500 or more.			
Date(s) Wages Paid	1st Month	2nd Month	3rd Month
Total deposits for quarter. Enter at line 10			
Signature	Title		Date

Fig. 4.3 - Simplified Version of Quarterly Form 941

headed: *Special Classes of Employment and Special Types of Payment.* Then look down the column headed: "Social Security and Medicare." There are approximately 75 entries in that table: far too many for us to discuss here.

Whatever the amount of taxable social security/medicare compensation there may be, the employee contributes 50% of the tax. You, as the employer, also contribute 50% of the tax. For this reason, you must take particular care to note the amount on line 8 in Figure 4.3. On the official Form 941, it is a different line number, which reads as: *Adjusted total of Social Security and Medicare taxes.* The 50% employer amount is deductible to you as a business expense.

There is one other item that we must caution you about in Figure 4.3. On lines 5 and 6 we show two separate tax rates (12.4% and 2.9%) which total 15.3%. These rates are for **example purposes** only. The social security/medicare tax rates are always subject to being increased. This is why it is so important that you get an updated Circular E every year (in January).

FTD "Coupons" Explained

Now that you have withheld and collected money from your employees, and have contributed 50% of their social security/ medicare tax, what do you do with this money? Do you forward it to the IRS, quarterly, when you file Form 941?

In most cases, "No."

Only when the amount withheld, or amount due, at the end of any quarter is less than $500, can you forward the money directly to the IRS. In all other cases, you must present the money — in cash, check, or money order — to an *authorized depository.* This generally is any commercial bank which is a member of the Federal Reserve System. But you just can't hand the money to them. You must use Form 8109: *Federal Tax Deposit Coupon* (FTD "coupons" for short).

There are special deposit rules which tell you when to use the FTD coupons. For details on these rules, we refer you again to Circular E. In general, if the withholdings are more than $500 but less than $3,000, you deposit monthly. If the withholdings are $3,000 or more, you make deposits weekly.

On each FTD coupon, there are entry boxes for indicating the type of tax and the tax period against which the deposit is to be applied. Take great care to mark the entry boxes properly. Otherwise, the deposit coupons will generate many computer mismatchings from bank to IRS, and from IRS to you. Any additional taxes due, or penalties asserted, fall on your shoulders: not on the "authorized" depository bank.

Even though you make your deposits to the bank on time, the bank may electronically report them late to the IRS. If this happens, there is a late payment penalty of 5% which you must pay. The same 5% penalty applies if you get disgusted with the bank and make your deposits directly with the IRS. Apparently there is some behind-the-scenes arrangement between the IRS and the Federal Reserve banks. You have no depository choice in the matter.

Additionally, another depository mandate exists. If the total of all required deposits (income tax withholdings, social security tax, medicare tax, and other employer taxes) exceeds $50,000 in any year, you must make *electronic deposits* for all subsequent years. This is the IRS's much heralded ***Electronic Federal Tax Payment System*** (EFTPS). Once you are required to make EFTPS deposits, any subsequent failure to do so is subject to a 10% penalty. All depository penalties are frustrating and irritating. You are not notified of them until six to 12 months after each deposit.

Fortunately, most states requiring employer quarterly returns are more reasonable than the IRS. Most allow direct mail-in at the time the quarterlies are filed. This is the more sensible way.

Still Another Form: 940

There is another federal employer form that you need to be aware of. This is Form 940: ***Federal Unemployment Tax Return.*** It is filed once a year. It is referred to as the FUTA form: the "A" is for annually.

The FUTA tax is approximately 6% of the first $7,000 in wages paid to each employee during the year. We say "approximately" (6% on $7,000) because these figures change slightly from year to year. The important point is that you — as the employer — have to pay this tax. It is not withheld from the employee's wages. It is a pure tax on you for the privilege of hiring workers. This is one reason why it is on a separate tax form of its own.

In virtually every state, you also have to pay unemployment tax. If you pay into a state unemployment fund timely, and in the proper amount, you are allowed a credit against the FUTA tax. This credit is approximately 5% of the first $7,000 in wages paid. The net effect is that the FUTA tax, after adjustment for state credits, is approximately 1% of the $7,000 wages paid. The end result, however, is that you pay unemployment tax to both state and federal authorities.

If your FUTA tax is more than $100 for the year, it must be deposited quarterly. You have to use the same FTD coupons that you use for depositing withholding taxes and social security taxes. If you have two or more employees for the year, each earning $7,000 or more, your FUTA tax will be over $100. If your undeposited FUTA tax is less than $100 at the end of the year, you may pay it directly to the IRS when filing Form 940.

Taxability of Fringe Benefits

The taxability of, and withholdings from, fringe benefits to employees are punitive aggravations to employers. Even as a small business employer, it is difficult to avoid entirely allowing certain fringe benefits to employees. Sick pay, prizes and awards, discounts on merchandise and services, meals and snacks on premises, use of company car, health plans, educational assistance, and so on, are customary practices by most employers. Some of these benefits are taxable and some are not. The distinction is not crystal clear.

The IRS position is that all fringes are taxable unless specifically designated as nontaxable by law. The rationale is that the fringe benefits are variant forms of compensation which are conferred only on employees. They are not conferred upon ordinary customers and clients of the business. Were they also allowed to customers and clients, as well as to employees, they would be construed as pure gifts . . . which are nontaxable. Once a fringe benefit is characterized as taxable, it is subject to income tax withholdings *and* to social security/medicare tax.

To help clear up the ambiguities, Section 132(a): *Exclusion From Gross Income* is particularly relevant. It says—

Gross income shall not include any fringe benefit which qualifies as a—
(1)   no-additional-cost service,
(2)   qualified employee discount,
(3)   working condition fringe,
(4)   de minimis fringe,
(5)   qualified transportation fringe, or
(6)   qualified moving expense reimbursement.

Other portions of Section 132 go to define these terms, and the limitations with respect to spouses, children, and parents of employees. Also included are treatment of certain eating facilities, qualified employee discounts, and parking on or near the business premises.

The essence of Section 132 (Certain Fringe Benefits) is that the benefits conferred must be essential to doing business. They must be necessary for carrying on the business, as opposed to some additional bonus to employees. For example, meals, snacks, and beverages furnished at the employer's place of business during public business hours are construed as "for convenience of the employer." In other words, by providing these items on premises, there is no disruption in the flow of business. Similarly for employee discounts on merchandise and services. So long as the discounts do not exceed profit markups or are comparable to those offered to the public for promotions and special sales, they are nontaxable.

Group health plans instituted under Section 106(a) are not taxable, provided there are no discriminatory benefits to "highly compensated" employees. Compensation for personal injuries or sickness are not taxable, provided the conditions in Section 104(a) are strictly met. There are exceptions for excess compensation over those amounts actually incurred for medical, dental, and pharmaceutical services. The nontaxable provisions apply to workmen's compensation (under state law), injury awards in lawsuits, and insurance payments for accidents, sickness, and illness.

Except for the above, virtually every other fringe benefit is taxable (IRS Reg. 1.61-21). For example, "sick pay" — which is the continuation of one's wages while sick — is fully taxable, if paid by the employer out of his business proceeds. The personal use of a company car (for commuting, for week-ends, or for vacations) is also fully taxable. The same applies to the use of any company facilities for personal lodging, transportation, entertainment, or recreation. The tax problem is determining the "fair market value" of these benefits for inclusion in each employee's gross pay. If an employer undervalues these benefits, he is subject to an excise tax (another penalty).

The taxability of fringe benefits is an onerous task for small businesses. We suggest, therefore, that you limit your employee benefits strictly to Section 132 working condition fringes and to Section 106 group health plans. Forego all other benefit programs. If the competition forces you to reconsider, offer, instead, a commensurate increase in each employee's base pay.

Business Expense Reimbursements

In some businesses, employees will incur legitimate expenses in furthering the business interests of the employer. The employer tax concern becomes: How should these expenses be reimbursed? Should the employee be given a "standard allowance," such as a car allowance, per diem, travel allowance, entertainment allowance? Or, should he be reimbursed dollar-for-dollar for the actual (substantiated) expenses incurred?

For small businesses, we highly recommend the dollar-for-dollar reimbursement method. Here's why.

Any standard allowance that you provide is fully tax reportable. It is "other compensation" to your employees. This means that it is subject to income tax withholding, and, in many cases, subject to social security tax withholdings also. This reportability and the withholdings are going to make your employees very unhappy. They'll have to justify their business expenses to the IRS, before any deductions (on their tax returns) will be allowed.

Commencing in 1987, the rules for employee business expense deduction have been tightened severely. To get any deduction at all, the expenses have to be classified into those which are reimbursed, and those which are not reimbursed. Separate tax forms are required for each. And before any business expense deduction form can be used, the employee must have perfect records. Every penny of expenditure must be positively documented. In practice, the new rules are inordinately unreasonable.

A far better way to go is the dollar-for-dollar reimbursement method. This, in tax jargon, is the *adequate-accounting-to-employer* rule. This rule says that where there is adequate expense accounting by the employee to his employer, and the employer reimburses the employee dollar for dollar, there is no taxability to the employee and no tax withholding by the employer. The term "adequate accounting" means that the employee submits a written expense voucher to the employer, with all supporting substantiation attached.

So that you know the dollar-for-dollar method is valid, let us cite the IRS regulatory language. We refer to Regulation 1.274-5A(e)(2)(i): *Reimbursements equal to expenses.* It reads—

For purposes of computing tax liability, an employee need not report on his tax return business expenses for travel, transportation, entertainment, gifts, or with respect to listed property paid or incurred by him solely for the benefit of his

*employer for which he is required to, and does, make an
adequate accounting to his employer and which are charged
directly or indirectly to the employer or for which the employee
is paid through advances, reimbursements, or otherwise,
provided that the total amount of such advances,
reimbursements, and charges is equal to such expenses.*

Obviously, there is no point in going through all of the tax
hassle if you can set up internal procedures to comply with
Regulation 1.274-5A(e)(2)(i). There is a simple way to do this.
Prepare your own expense voucher forms, or select among those
preprinted forms commercially available. Then instruct your
employees to submit their vouchers to you on whatever periodic
basis is appropriate for the expenses incurred.

After examining the vouchers for reasonableness and legitimacy,
reimburse the employee by check for the exact amount approved.
Code this check in accordance with our discussions in Chapter 3
(Figure 3.3, particularly). This way, you get a business tax
deduction for the expense. Best of all, it is not tax reportable by
your employee(s).

Getting Out Those W-2s

There's one chore each year that you probably already know
about. It's getting out those Form W-2s. In case you haven't
scrutinized a W-2 lately, its official heading is: *Wage and Tax
Statement.* This is the summary form that you must prepare and
present to each employee, on or before January 31 of each year.

To alert you to a few key points in preparing a W-2, we present
an abbreviated version of the form in Figure 4.4. Note that we
purposely have emphasized Boxes 1, 12, 13, and 14.

Box 1 is labeled: *Wages, tips, other compensation.* This box is
where you enter the gross annual remuneration to an employee,
whether subject to withholdings or not. The amount entered must
be the grand total of all cash, check, and noncash payments. This
means that Box 1 includes not only what is normally considered
wages and tips, but every form of "other compensation." This is
where employee confusion will arise.

The term "other compensation" includes all taxable fringe
benefits, unvouchered travel reimbursements, car allowances,
expense allowances, use of company property and services, excess
employee discounts, sick pay, bonuses, prizes, awards, life

Form W-2	Wage and Tax Statement		Year
EMPLOYER'S ID	1 Wages, etc. & other compensation	2 Federal income tax withheld	
EMPLOYER'S Name, address, ZIP	3 Soc. Sec. wages	4 Soc. Sec. tax withheld	
	5 Medicare wages	6 Medicare tax withheld	
	7 Soc. Sec. tips	8 Allocated tips	
EMPLOYEE'S ID	9 EIC payments	10 Dependent care	
EMPLOYEE'S Name, address, ZIP	11 Nonqual plans	12 Benefits in Box 1	
	13 See instructions	14 Other	
Copy C - for - EMPLOYEE'S RECORDS	15 Pension plans, etc. ☐	☐☐☐☐☐☐	

16 State	Employer's State ID	17 State Wages, etc.	18 State Income Tax	19 Locality	20 Local Wages, etc.	21 Local Income Tax

Fig. 2.1 - Edited/Abbreviated Version of Form W-2 for Employees

insurance premiums, and so on. Since these items are not paid regularly throughout the year like wages, most employees tend to forget about them. They are shocked when Box 1 shows an amount greater than their normal wages. They will argue that you overstated the Box 1 amount. They will insist that you provide them promptly with an itemized breakdown. Otherwise, they will complain to some government agency.

Fortunately, there are Boxes 12, 13, and 14 on Form W-2. In Box 12, you enter the total value of all taxable fringe benefits in Box 1. Box 13 enables you to enter up to three different code symbols from a preprinted choice of 15 (in the instructions for preparing Form W-2). If more than three code symbols are required, you are authorized to prepare a supplemental statement to Box 13. Box 14 is for listing any other information you want to impart to each employee.

It is not our intention to tell you how to prepare the W-2 forms. Ample official instructions are available for this purpose. We do want you to be aware, however, of Boxes 2, 4, and 6. Box 2 is the total federal income tax that you withheld. Box 4 is the total social security tax that you withheld. Box 6 is the total medicare tax that you withheld. You must reconcile these three totals with those quarterly employer returns that you filed throughout the year. There will be parallel reconciliations for any state, city, or local withholdings that you made.

Altogether, you have to prepare at least six copies of each W-2 for each employee. The official copy sequence is as follows:

Copy A – to Social Security Administration
Copy B – to employee for filing with Federal return
Copy C – to employee for his/her own tax records
Copy D – to be retained by employer (you)
Copy 1 – to State, City, or Local Tax Department
Copy 2 – to employee for filing with Local return(s)

[Sometimes multiple "Copy 2s" are required, one each for State, City, Regional, or Local income tax returns.]

If an employee loses or destroys his set of W-2s (copies B, C, and 2), you have the choice of redoing a set and marking it "Reissued," or, you can make three photocopies of your Copy D, and re-mark them as Copy B, Copy C, and Copy 2.

If an employee stops working for you before the end of the year, you have 30 days after the termination to furnish him (or her) Copies B, C, and 2. Or, if the employee consents, you can wait until you prepare the W-2s for all of your employees. However, be sure that you have every terminated employee's latest mailing address. Otherwise, you'll be getting frantic phone calls and letters as April 15th approaches.

5

COLLECTING SALES TAX

There Are 45 States Which Levy A Sales Tax. This Tax Is Imposed On Tangible Personal Property Which Is Used, Stored, Rented, Or Otherwise Consumed Within Each State. As A Retailer, You Apply For A "Seller's Permit" . . . And Become Deputized As A Tax Collector. Not All Sales Are Taxable, However. The Two Most Common Exemptions Are Sales To Out-Of-State Customers And Sales To Other Retailers For Resale. Periodically, You Are Required To File "Sales And Use Tax Returns" And Remit Promptly The Full Amount Of Tax. Preparing These Sales Tax Returns Requires Good Supporting Records For Taxable Sales, Tax Receipts, and Nontaxable Sales.

The sales tax is a primary source of revenue for most states and local authorities, even for those which impose an income tax. For those states which impose no income tax, the sales tax is particularly pervasive. It applies to virtually every business transaction in the retail market. We say "virtually" because there are some exceptions . . . but not very many.

In theory, the sales tax applies to the retailer for the privilege of selling commodities, goods, and services. In practice, it is the one tax which is allowed to be passed through to the ultimate consumer. As a consequence of this pass through, it is more widely recognized as a *consumption* tax. Thus, the person or entity who buys an item for his/her/its own use and/or consumption winds up paying the tax directly. In other words, the sales tax is now generally recognized as a pure "add-on" to the regular sales price of an item. This is not the case with other taxes which businesses must endure.

There are 45 states plus the District of Columbia which impose the sales tax. (The nonimposers are Alaska, Delaware, Montana, New Hampshire, and Oregon.) The sales tax laws and collection burdens are not uniform throughout all 45 (plus D.C.) states. Different items are taxed, different services are taxed, and different exceptions apply. For instructional purposes, however, we must pick one state as being sort of representative. For this purpose, we will use the state of California. It has one of the highest and most complex sales tax structures of any state. It provides a good example of the burdens imposed on a new business owner, as a deputy tax collector.

Applies to Retailers Only

When you go into any new business, you need to know which transactions are subject to your collecting the sales tax. Whether you collect or not collect depends on your type of business. If you are a manufacturer, wholesaler, grower, producer, broker, consultant, or other nonretailer, the sales tax may not apply to you. If you are a retailer, it definitely applies.

In general, the sales tax applies to the gross receipts of retailers from the sale of tangible personal property. This *excludes* real property, securities in all forms (which are intangibles), personal services (such as repair, installation, and consultation), and certain statutory items such as food, medicine, and insurance. The tax applies to certain rentals such as video items, equipment, vehicles, and rooms. It applies when a customer furnishes the raw materials and you furnish the fabrication labor to produce an end-product for that customer. It applies to advertising material, art work, film processing, storage facilities, and to any other tangible personal property purchased from a retailer.

The central question of concern is: Who is a retailer?

Answer: A retailer is anyone who makes more than two *retail sales* in a 12-month period. This eliminates the occasional sale by one consumer to another, where the seller is not regularly engaged in retail business. Auctioneers, liquidators, and others disposing of personal property items in multiple sales — even though not normally thought of as retailers — are "retailers" for sales tax collection purposes.

A "retail sale" is defined as a sale for any purpose other than resale. This applies to all transactions in the regular course of business involving tangible personal property items. Because a retail sale is defined as "any sale other than resale," there is a presumption that every sale is a taxable sale unless it can be established that it is a resale.

The sales tax applies to the gross receipts from a retail sale, and is included therein. This means that the "sales price" to which the tax applies includes all receipts, whether in the form of cash, credit, property, service, or barter of any kind. In other words, a retailer does not collect sales tax simply on the amount of cash that he receives. He collects it on the full consideration that constitutes the sales price, whether cash or noncash. The sales tax itself, however, must be subsequently remitted to the designated state agency by check or money order. This tends to put a damper on noncash forms of business.

Collection at "Point of Sale"

If a taxable item passes from one retailer to another, and then to another where the consumer takes delivery: Which one collects the sales tax?

It is the *point of sale* retailer who collects the sales tax. This is the retailer who makes all of the contractual arrangements for the sale. He is the one who informs the customer of the final sales price, payment terms, delivery terms, and warranties (if any). He is the one who legally joins the seller and buyer together, and against whom complaints of product malperformance (if any) are lodged. This is the "point of sale" retailer because of the contractual binding involved.

Other retailers in the chain, such as one acquiring the item and a completely different one making the delivery, are simply agents for the point of sale retailer. The associated retailers may each get a commission on the sale. If they do, it is added to the sales price on which the sales tax applies.

Delivery costs from the point of sale are not part of the sales price. This is because there would be different sales prices, for the same item, depending on where a customer lived, or where he directed that it be sent. Besides, a customer always has the right to pick up the item on his own at the point of sale. Delivery costs to the customer, therefore, are not subject to the sales tax.

Why are we discussing the point of sale issue? Isn't this self-evident?

"Yes," ordinarily. But, "No," in reality.

If the rate of sales tax and the items to which it applied were exactly uniform throughout every county of the state, throughout every state of the United States, and in every country of the world, there would be no point of sale issue. But there is no such uniformity. Even in the state of California, different counties impose different sales tax rates . . . for different revenue purposes.

Consumers sometimes try to take advantage of the non-uniformity of sales tax rates. They may place an order in one sales tax jurisdiction, take delivery in a second jurisdiction, but actually use the item in a third jurisdiction. To discourage this, the point of sale principle prevails. This principle, however, is limited strictly to in-state transactions. One state of jurisdiction cannot control the revenue collected in another state's jurisdiction.

Out-of-state transactions pose another problem, especially for small businesses. If you have one or two customers in each of the 45 taxing states other than you own, are you going to keep track of all of their sales tax requirements, and collect taxes for them? Of course you're not! If your customer does indeed live out-of-state, ignore the sales tax and treat the transaction as a nontaxable sale.

In fact, California—one of the toughest sales tax states of all— treats sales to out-of-state consumers as exempt from the sales tax. To do otherwise would create horrible overlapping disputes between different state jurisdictions. Instead, California imposes a "use tax" on out-of-state purchases delivered in-state, and a few other states do the same. The California use tax rate is identical to its sales tax rate.

To enforce the use tax collection process, California has a "deemed-in-state" rule. Any out-of-state retailer selling to California residents is deemed to be engaged in business in California if he has any kind of branch office, sales representative, or subsidiary agent located in California. Having interstate branch offices and sales agents is not the most likely organization structure of a small business just starting up. Therefore, we urge that small businesses collect the sales-use tax only when it is proper and convenient to do so. Do not go out of your way to be a determined sales-use tax collector unless you really want to work for state government(s) full time (at no pay!).

Seller's Permit Required

How do you become deputized as a sales tax collector?

You apply for a *seller's permit*. You apply to the nearest branch office of the sales tax agency in the state where you principally do business. In California, the applicable agency is the State Board of Equalization, Department of Business Taxes. In other states, there are comparably-named agencies which enforce sales tax collection.

You apply not so much for a permit as you do for *registration*. The permit is a registration of the fact that you are a retailer. As such, you are assigned an Account Number. This account number is used for computer-policing and audit-policing your sales tax collections . . . and conveyances to the state.

You pay no fee for a seller's permit. The obvious reason is that when the permit is issued, you become a deputy tax collector for the state. If you paid a fee, you would expect some services from the state. It's the other way around. You are performing services for the state. Your only recognition is that you pay no fee for the privilege of doing so.

An example version of a Seller's Permit is presented in Figure 5.1. Note that it is valid until revoked or cancelled (when you cease doing business). Since it is not a for-fee license, it is not transferable to a successor business. If you have more than one retail business location, you need a separate seller's permit for each location. As long as your business name and form do not change, your Account Number remains the same for all of your business outlets (in the issuing state).

Application for a seller's permit usually requires your appearance in person. This is because a state agent needs to witness your signature. But, before you apply, we suggest that you phone the sales tax agency and request that the pertinent information and applicable forms be mailed to you. This is to give you time to study the material before casting yourself in sales tax concrete. You want to avoid frequent changes in the information that you give to the issuing agency. In California, the document that you are expected to complete in person is—

Application for Seller's Permit and
Registration as a Retailer

Among the registration information sought from you are the following:

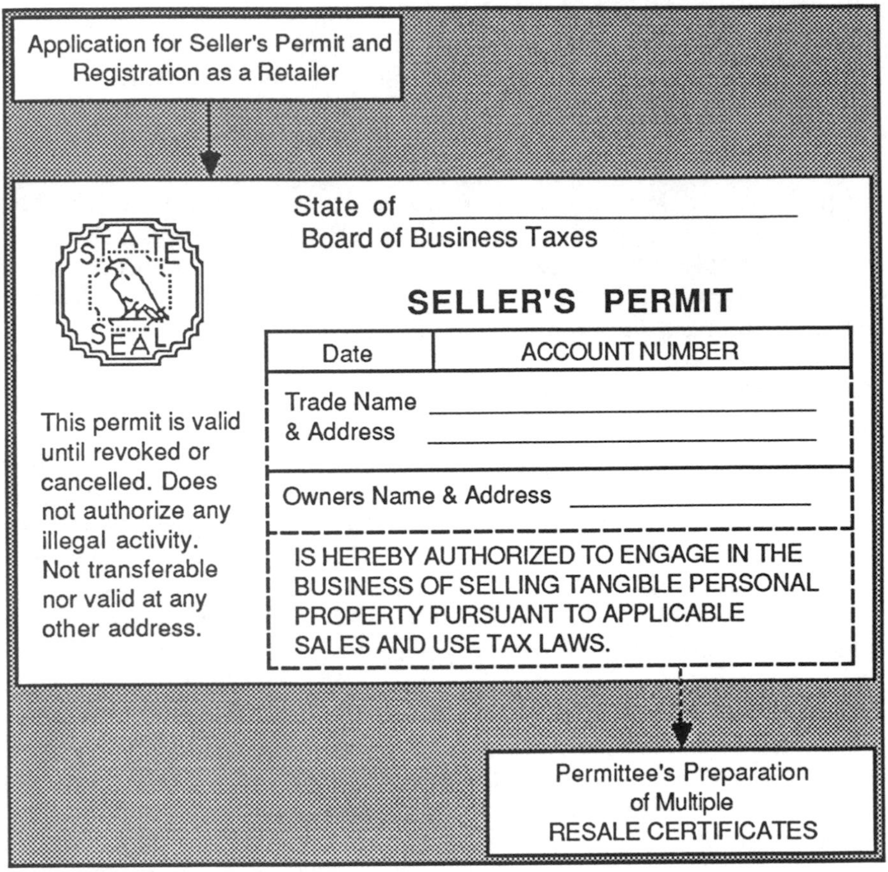

Application for Seller's Permit and
Registration as a Retailer

State of _____
Board of Business Taxes

SELLER'S PERMIT

Date	ACCOUNT NUMBER

Trade Name _____
& Address _____

Owners Name & Address _____

IS HEREBY AUTHORIZED TO ENGAGE IN THE
BUSINESS OF SELLING TANGIBLE PERSONAL
PROPERTY PURSUANT TO APPLICABLE
SALES AND USE TAX LAWS.

This permit is valid
until revoked or
cancelled. Does
not authorize any
illegal activity.
Not transferable
nor valid at any
other address.

Permittee's Preparation
of Multiple
RESALE CERTIFICATES

Fig. 5.1 - Example "Seller's Permit" and Related Matters

1. Trade name of your business
2. Principal location (head office)
3. Other retail location(s), if any
4. Type of organization:
   ☐ Proprietorship ☐ Partnership ☐ Corporation ☐ Other
5. Nature of business (what are you selling?)
6. Your principal activity:
   ☐ Manufacturing ☐ Wholesaling ☐ Retailing ☐ Repairing
   ☐ Personal servicing ☐ Renting ☐ Contracting ☐ Other
7. Exact date business started
8. Estimated gross sales, first year

9. Number, type, and payroll of employees
10. Your Federal I.D. Number (of course)

You want to be properly prepared when you apply for your seller's permit. Above all, however, do not be overly optimistic about your first year gross sales. Deliberately keep your estimated sales low. Otherwise, you'll have to make a prepayment of the entire first year's estimated sales tax! This prepayment is upfront money which will be held by the issuing agency as a *surety bond* to assure performance of your collection and remittance. You may not get it back, nor be allowed a tax credit for it, for many years.

Importance of Resale Certificates

A sale for resale is exempt from tax. This means that even if you are a registered retailer and you engage in resales to another retailer, there is no tax collection obligation on your part. The same applies if you purchase items from another retailer: he does not have to collect sales tax from you. It is the retailer dealing with the ultimate consumer/user who collects the sales tax. All other intermediate steps between producer and consumer are treated as "resales."

The mechanism by which resales are not taxed is the *resale certificate* . This certificate is prepared and rendered by each holder of a seller's permit. It is not prepared by a state agency as in the case of the seller's permit itself. Furthermore, there is no one resale certificate. Multiple certificates — as many as necessary — may be prepared by a valid permit holder. These resale permits, provided they are prepared in good faith, are prima facie evidence of transactions involving resales. The functional scheme of these certificates in the business of reselling of tangible personal property is presented in Figure 5.2. If you sell items to other retailers, you must keep their resale certificates in your files at all times. Like the official permit itself, resale certificates are valid until revoked or cancelled.

Each state has its own format and wording for its resale certification. We suggest that you acquire a batch of official forms and have them readily available. For those situations where you are the buyer (for resale), you could have some of the forms filled-out and ready to go. The essential information to be entered is the Account Number on your seller's permit, your Federal I.D. Number, the trade name (and location) of your business, the general

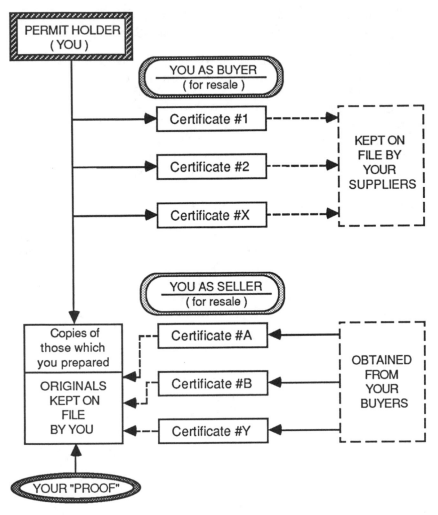

Fig. 5.2 - Exemption Role of Resale Certificates

class of customers to whom you expect to sell, and a certification that you will not use the items acquired for your personal, family, or business benefit.

This raises the question: What about those personal property items that are used in the business itself, and not immediately resold to other retailers or to the consumer public?

Except for demonstration models and display samples, all property items used in your business are subject to the sales tax. You pay the sales tax out of your otherwise gross proceeds as part of your cost of doing business. We are addressing now, particularly, such items as furniture, fixtures, tools, equipment, materials, parts, supplies, machinery, vehicles, and other things used in the business. After all, you are the consumer/user of these items if they are not acquired with the intention of immediately offering them for resale.

The only exceptions to this "immediate resale" rule are demonstration models and display samples. If these items are subsequently sold as used property, the sales tax is collected at that time. If the demonstrators and displays become damaged, worn out, or obsolete, and if they are junked, destroyed, or given away, there is no sales tax. Obviously, there has been no sale. However, any demonstration or display property loaned to a customer for trial purposes or during repairs is subject to a sales tax on the fair rental value of such loaners.

Other Exempt Transactions

Up to this point, we have touched on only two types of exempt transactions. These are sales to out-of-state customers and in-state resales. There are a host of other exempt transactions, too numerous for us to discuss here. Which sales are exempt and which are nonexempt vary from state to state. All states do have one feature in common. They "presume" that all sales are taxable unless *you* can establish that they are nontaxable. You need to do your homework to identify those transactions which are statutorily exempt in your state.

To give you one simple example of the homework needed on your part, take food and food products. Most states exempt food products if they are bought in packaged form and taken home by the consumer, where they are prepared for eating. But if food is bought and eaten in a restaurant, or at a fast-food outlet, it is subject to sales tax. What about candy, cookies, beverages, and over-the-counter medicines? Are these packaged food products, or are they taxable items like cigarettes and lighter fluid? Alcoholic beverages (liquor, beer, wine) are not only sales taxed, but are "sin taxed" as well.

Another simple example. Some states tax clothing only if the sale amount exceeds from $75 to $175. Other states (like California) tax all clothing. Some states tax gas and electricity if it exceeds a certain minimum amount per month. All states, however, tax gasoline . . . doubly and triply.

Most states do not tax items sold to bona fide church organizations, public school districts, U.S. government agencies, in-state agencies, invalid and handicapped persons, and foreign dignitaries under diplomatic agreements. Many states also do not tax repair and installation labor, professional services (medical, legal, accounting), advertisements (radio, TV, newspaper), and other "public purpose" activities.

There is a message here that we are trying to get across. Each business in its own state of jurisdiction has its own characteristic exempt transactions. Therefore, each entrepreneur should make sure that he knows intimately and understands thoroughly which of his transactions are sales tax exempt. Detailed rulings and interpretations thereon usually can be obtained from the sales tax agency which issues the sellers' permits.

Periodic Returns Required

At some point, all sales tax collections have to be remitted to the state-designated enforcement agency. This is done at prescribed periodic intervals. Accompanying each remittance, an official **Sales and Use Tax Return** has to be prepared.

Generally, these returns are filed on a quarterly basis (similar to employer quarterly returns). For businesses whose taxable sales are more than $20,000 per month, monthly returns typically are required. For businesses whose taxable sales are less than $2,000 per year, annual returns are required.

When quarterly returns are made, monthly prepayments are required. You cannot hold the money to earn interest on it. It has to be turned over to the state more or less continuously. Some states, such as California, require full prepayment in the quarterly month which coincides with the ending month of the state's fiscal year (June 30 for California). Otherwise, full payment is required on or before the last day of the month following the quarterly period.

At the time your seller's permit is issued, you will be handed certain written instructions and regulations. There is one such instruction you can count on, no matter in which state you are doing business. For California, this instruction reads—

Sales must be reported on returns made to the Board at such time and for such periods as the Board may require. A return must be filed for each period even though no taxable sales were made during such period. Each return must be accompanied by a remittance for the amount of tax due. REMIT BY CHECK OR MONEY ORDER. DO NOT SEND CASH OR STAMPS.

An edited version of a California sales and use tax return is presented in Figure 5.3. We have tried to highlight the key features thereof, so that you will be instructed ahead of time. Note particularly the itemized deductions for exempt transactions. Also note the separate computational sections for county/local taxes and for special district taxes. At the bottom of each return you are told:

Always Write Your Account Number on Your Check or Money Order

At the bottom of Figure 5.3, also note the line labeled: **Amount Due and Payable.** This means that you compute the full tax and pay it, whether you collected the correct amount or not. If you have under-collected, you are losing money. If you have over-collected, you may be losing customers.

Good Supporting Records Needed

Collecting sales tax is a burdensome task. Especially when you have to remit the money so promptly after collecting it. In the rush to get the returns in on time, mistakes can be made. Often, the proper amount of tax is overpaid.

All sales tax authorities take a commonly-held hard position. They assert that everything you sell (including services) is taxable, unless you can establish otherwise. "Establishing otherwise" requires good records, consistently kept, month after month. If you records are sloppy, you put yourself at risk of paying taxes—out of your own pocket—on sales which are not taxable.

To typify the kind of records needed, we quote from California instructions to permittees:

Every seller, retailer, and person storing, using or otherwise consuming in this State tangible personal property purchased from a retailer, and every lessor and lessee of tangible personal property for use in this State, shall keep adequate and complete records showing—

State of California
SALES AND USE TAX RETURN

Due Date ▶		Account Number ▶	
For period ending		Permittee: _____	
		_____	
State, County, Local, District		_____	

			FOR STATE USE
1.	TOTAL GROSS SALES		
2.	Purchases other than for resale		
3.	TOTAL : Add lines 1 and 2		
	EXEMPT TRANSACTIONS		
4.	Sales for resale		
5.	Food & food products		
6.	Repair & installation labor		
7.	Sales to U.S. Government		
8.	Sales out-of-state		
9.	Sales tax in line 1		
10.	Returns & allowances		
a.	other exempt transactions :		
b.	Explain :		
11.	Total Exempt Transactions: lines 4 through 10 b		
12.	NET TAXABLE SALES: subtract 11 from 3		

Computation of Tax : See Instructions	State :	Line 12 x _____ % ➡	
	County :	Line 12 x _____ % ➡	
	Local :	Line 12 x _____ % ➡	
	District :	Line 12 x _____ % ➡	

Record of prepayments (if any)	TOTAL TAX	
	Subtract Prepayments	
Computation of penalty & interest (if any)	AMOUNT DUE AND PAYABLE	

Signature	Title	Date

Fig. 5.3 - Edited Version of California Sales Tax Return

(1)   Gross receipts from sales or rental payments from leases of tangible personal property (including any services that are part of the sale or lease) made within California irrespective of whether the seller or lessor regards the receipts as taxable or nontaxable.

(2)   All deductions allowed by law and claimed in filing returns.

(3)   Total purchase price of all tangible personal property purchased for sale or consumption or lease in California.

*These records must include the normal books of account **ordinarily maintained** by the **average prudent business-man** engaged in the activity in question, together with all bills, receipts, invoices, cash register tapes, or other documents of original entry supporting the entries in the books of account as well as all schedules and working papers used in connection with the preparation of tax returns.* [Emphasis added.]

Whew! This is a tall order. It defines the kind of perfection demanded, but allows you a way out. It permits you to keep only those records which are "ordinarily maintained" . . . by the "average prudent businessman." We assume that you are a prudent business-person who does not want to become a slave to record-keeping.

Good Invoicing Design

At the very least, you want to have some kind of gross sales/receipts ledger. On this ledger, you want to be able to distinguish between your sales receipts and your tax receipts. You also want to be able to distinguish between taxable sales and nontaxable sales. This is where a good invoicing design of your sales receipts can be helpful.

When starting a new business, you may want to design your sales invoices in a format that permits distinction between taxable and nontaxable sales. For example, at the heading of your invoices you could have check boxes such as:

      ☐ Taxable sale
         ☐ applicable rate _____%
      ☐ Nontaxable sale
         ☐ exemption code _____

The "exemption code" could be a footnote-type listing (or highlighted box) which cross-references to the exemption statute(s) of your state. It could also cross-reference to the exempt transactions listed on your state's sales tax return (as per Fig. 5.3).

After formulating your own exemption code system, it is not a bad idea to have it reviewed by a state sales tax official. Such a person will not give you a written approval or other certification of your listing, but he may at least give you a verbal O.K.

Having your exempt transactions properly identified will prove tremendously helpful in minimizing customer complaints for any overcollecting of the sales tax. Distinguishing between taxable sales, tax receipts, and nontaxable sales will also prove helpful when preparing your sales tax returns and gross sales/receipts ledger.

At this point you should particularly note line 10 in Figure 5.3 which is captioned "Returns & allowances." The phrase *returns and allowances* addresses those rather unpleasant aspects of handling receipted money. If a customer or client becomes dissatisfied, his money often has to be returned. In this same category are customer checks or credit-card charges which "bounce." In some situations, you may allow a credit or give a refund to sweeten a complaint against you. You may also provide sales incentives in the form of up-front discounts. All of these matters are legitimate adjustments (subtractions) from the total gross sales reported. This "adjustment" is a business necessity: an obvious form of exemption from sales tax. Ordinarily, returns and allowances comprise a small percentage of your gross sales and receipts.

Another necessary adjustment — frequently overlooked by new businesses — is the amount of sales tax included in gross receipts. If the sales tax is included in the reported total receipts, one can wind up paying sales tax on the sales tax *and* income tax on the sales tax. This can happen because "gross receipts" means the total of all monies coming into the business, including sales tax collections. Obviously, you need careful record-keeping to "back out" the sales tax from your gross sales.

6

COST OF GOODS SOLD

There Are "Direct Costs" Associated With The Purchasing And/Or Producing Of Goods And Services Sold To Customers. These Costs Become Your First Major Subtraction From Your Gross Receipts. The Two Most Tax-Questioned Items Are Cost Of Labor And Ending Inventory. There Are Two Forms Of Direct Labor: Employees (Form W-2) And Nonemployees (Form 1099-MISC). Be Sure To Distinguish Between Them. Your Ending Inventory Is "Tied-Up" Capital; It Provides You No Tax Benefits. The Higher Your Ending Inventory, The Higher The Tax On Your Net Profit.

In this chapter, we want to bring into focus your "Gross receipts or sales" enterable on the first line of your federal income tax returns. The idea is that if you are in an ongoing business, you have to tax-account for all monies received from your customers and clients. This includes your sales income, service income, rental income, and other income that you derive directly from the consuming public. All of this constitutes your gross receipts in the business.

From your gross receipts, you are allowed to make adjustments (subtractions) for "returns and allowances" and for any sales tax collections in your gross receipts.

We come now to another off-the-top adjustment (subtraction) from your gross receipts. In fact, it is — or can be — quite a major deduction in itself. This adjustment is called officially: **Cost of**

goods sold. We prefer the more explicit term "cost of goods & services sold." These are your direct costs of doing business. They are *direct* in the sense that these are costs that you pay to others for property or services that go directly to your customers and clients.

There is no limit on the deductibility of your direct costs, so long as you can substantiate them with good and adequate records. We will comment on record-keeping as we go along. But our main purpose here is to have you recognize and understand what your direct costs are.

The Sequence of Income

There are three terms that are tax confusing when operating a business. These terms are (1) Gross Receipts, (2) Gross Profit, and (3) Total Income. They all apply to the *income* portion of your federal tax returns. They apply whether you are a proprietorship, partnership, or corporation.

There is no use trying to define each of these terms in words alone. That will only add to the confusion. Instead, we will show the sequence in which they appear. This way, you can compare the terms and sense for yourself why they are chosen for what they are. We will ignore for the time being the actual phraseology used on the official tax forms.

The sequence that we want you to become familiar with is:

1. **Gross receipts** or sales   _____
   (derived from customers & clients)
2. Returns and allowances   _____
   (including any sales tax in line 1)
3. Adjusted gross receipts   _____
   (*subtract* line 2 from line 1)
4. Cost of goods sold   _____
   (that go directly to customers & clients)
5. **Gross profit**   _____
   (*subtract* line 4 from line 3)
6. Other income   _____
   (which is not in line 1)
7. **Total income**   _____
   (*add* lines 5 and 6)

This sequence tells you that you arrive at "gross profit" before you arrive at "total income." This may not sound right, but it is. Keep in mind that we are concerned with tax accounting: not ordinary cash flow.

From your gross receipts from customers, you subtract your direct cost of goods and services sold to those customers. This gives you a gross profit figure. (In some cases, this could be a loss instead of a profit.) To your gross profit you add "other income." This is income which is not derived directly from your customers and clients. It represents such monies as various refunds, insurance reimbursements, deposit returns, referral fees, incidental commissions, investment income, sales and trade-ins of assets used in the business, and so on.

Your "total income," therefore, is the sum of your gross profit (or loss) and other business income. It is from this total income that you subtract your administrative and indirect expenses to arrive at your net profit (or loss). We are not going to discuss your net profit (or loss) in this chapter. We want to focus here strictly on the direct cost of goods and services sold to your customers and clients.

The "Direct Cost" Subschedule

One's direct cost in doing business with customers is not a simple, one-line entry item. It consists of several entries — **eight** to be exact. Because all eight direct cost entries are not applicable to every business, a separate subschedule is provided on each federal tax form. The official words used vary slightly depending on the form of business: proprietorship, partnership, or corporation.

Because this is an instructional guide and not a tax forms preparation guide, we present our edited version of a direct cost subschedule. This we do in Figure 6.1. After reading through the sequence and line items in Figure 6.1, we urge that you mark or flag it in some manner. You want to be able to come back to it easily. We will be referring to it numerous times as we go along.

In all cases, the different federal tax forms identify the Figure 6.1 subschedule as: Cost of Goods Sold. On Form 1040 (proprietorship), it is identified as Part III, Schedule C; on Form 1065 (partnership), it is identified as Schedule A; and on Form 1120 (corporation), it is also identified as Schedule A. Though functionally a "subschedule," it is a means for summarizing all direct, off-the-top costs for doing business.

On Your Federal Income Tax Return			
	Subschedule on Forms 1040, 1065, and 1120		
COST OF GOODS & SERVICES SOLD			
1	Inventory : Beginning of year	1	
2	Purchases for resale	2	
3	Raw materials & supplies	3	
4	Fabrication Labor	4	
5	Other direct costs (explain)	5	
6	Subtotal : ADD lines 1 through 5	6	
7	Inventory : End of year	7	
8	SUBTRACT line 7 from line 6	8	
	and enter on designated income line	▼	▼
	COST OF GOODS & SERVICES SOLD ▶		

Fig. 6.1 - Cost of Goods/Services Sold to Customers/Clients

The phrase "cost of goods sold" has a direct impact on the profitability of your business The term "goods sold" is certainly quite clear. It means those goods (and services) **sold to your customers**. This obviously includes purchases for resale, but not those purchases used in-house in the business (such as tools, fixtures, machinery, equipment). Yet, the word "cost" implies all costs — including purchases used in-house — associated with goods sold. This is just not the case.

We think the complete phrase: "Cost of goods and services sold to customers and clients" would be more descriptive of your direct costs. But this is too long. So, we have shortened it to "Cost of Goods & Services." As long as you understand that it means *sold to your customers*, there should be no problem.

Those items of cost which do not go directly to your customers are your "indirect costs." We'll go into your indirect costs (and administrative expenses) in later chapters. Right now, all we want you to be thinking of is—

Direct cost . . . of goods and services
. . . sold to customers (and clients).

This is what Figure 6.1 is intended to detail. Let us discuss each of those line entries separately.

Beginning/Ending Inventories

Lines 1 and 7 of Figure 6.1 use the term "inventory." Line 1 is beginning inventory; line 7 is ending inventory. The "beginning" refers to the beginning of the tax year; "ending," of course, refers to the end of the tax year. The term "inventory" means merchandise intended for customers on hand at the beginning/ending of each tax year. It includes purchases for resale, finished and partly finished goods, raw materials, and fabrication/shipping supplies that become part of the merchandise you intend to sell.

Between the beginning and ending inventories of a given year, there will be a number of "adjustments" (additions and subtractions). Among these are new purchases, newly finished goods, new contract services, mark-ups for price increases by your suppliers, mark-downs for long-held inventory on hand, and write-offs for merchandise destroyed or stolen. You may want to discontinue a certain line of goods, and auction it off. If any of your inventory is obsolete or damaged, you may want to junk it or give it away. Whatever you do, record your adjustments in a methodical and systematic way. Do this as you go along; do not wait until the end of the year to record your adjustments.

Preferably, make your adjustments during the slow periods of your business year. Adjustments made exactly on your beginning/ending inventory days give the impression that you are "fudging." As a consequence, all last-minute beginning/ending inventory changes are tax suspect.

Your ending inventory of one year becomes the beginning inventory of the following year. These two figures should match exactly. Consequently, for tax purposes, you need "take" only one inventory, namely: that at year end. The ending dollar figure that you show on the tax form should be documented by actual physical count of each merchandise category.

Purchases for Resale

Good inventory accounting starts with good record-keeping when you purchase merchandise for resale. When you make such purchases — at least the first time — you have to provide a resale certificate to each of your suppliers. We discussed this in Chapter 5 (recall Fig. 5.2). The preparation and giving of resale certificates should prompt you into a systematic method for keeping track of all of your resale purchases. This certainly includes those billing invoices that your suppliers send to you. These invoices are your best evidence of inventory costs and changing wholesale values.

Prudence and care are required in your purchasing procedures. This is because only your purchases for resale (line 2 in Fig. 6.1) contribute to your direct costs. In any business, you'll be making other purchases besides those for resale. You must segregate all other purchases from those for resale. This can pose a problem — if you let it — when you purchase resale and nonresale items from the same supplier(s). If you make mixed purchases, we strongly suggest you issue **two** purchase orders: one for resale items and one for nonresale items. If you start in the habit of doing things right, you can avoid many tax-accounting problems down the line. As owner/manager of a small business, you will be confronted with these problems . . . sooner or later.

Take additional steps to insure that none of your "purchases for resale" are indeed consumed by you and your family, or are used in your business by yourself and your employees. Food, clothing, and hardware items are commonly used this way. Good self-discipline is required to sort these *personal use* items out, and adjust (downward) your purchases accordingly. You must make this adjustment before making your year-total entry on line 2.

There are several other potential adjustments to your purchases for resale. There are trade discounts, cash discounts, returns and allowances, and price adjustments. A "trade discount" is the difference between the supplier's list price of an article and the actual price that you pay. Many suppliers offer a "cash discount" if you pay within five to ten days or so. If you have to return any merchandise, for whatever reason, you'll be given a refund or allowed a credit in some form. Between the time of your purchase and your resale, there could be price adjustments by your supplier(s). All of these adjustments, plus others as appropriate, have to be made to your resale purchases to truly reflect your direct costs.

Our suggestion is that you make purchase adjustments directly on the respective purchase invoices to which they apply. Then on each invoice (in a color of your choice) highlight your net purchase cost. Try to keep the invoices in sequential order. This will make it easier for you to summarize your total true *purchase-for-resale* costs for the year.

Raw Materials & Supplies

Purchases for resale imply the acquisition of finished or semi-finished goods. There is another category of purchases for resale called "raw materials and supplies." These purchases consist of parts, materials, chemicals, containers, and other miscellaneous items needed for fabricating and finishing products for sale. These are another segment of costs which go into one's inventory of offerings to the public.

Because of the unfinished nature of raw materials and supplies, these items are not as subject to personal use sidetrackings as are the purchases for resale above. In businesses where parts and raw materials are used to fabricate finished or semi-finished goods, there is so much waste, defective parts, and scrap material lying around. Whether you use some of the raw materials for personal purposes or not, the adjustment effect on direct costs is negligible compared to the waste material thrown away.

There can be some confusion, however, over the term "supplies." Taxwise, there are two classes of supplies. There are direct-cost supplies and indirect-cost supplies. The direct supplies are those used in the fabrication, storage, preparation, and shipping of goods to customers. Indirect supplies are such items as office supplies, small tools, cleaning solvents, stationery, and the like. To distinguish between the two classes, *shop* supplies comprise your direct costs whereas office supplies are indirect costs. It is the shop supplies which are included in the entry on line 3 (of Fig. 6.1).

By comparing the magnitude of the entries on lines 2 (purchases for resale) and 3 (materials and supplies), one can ascertain the primary nature of the business. If line 2 is larger than line 3, it is primarily a sales (and service) type business. If line 3 is larger than line 2, it is primarily a manufacturing (and producing) business. If line 2 is blank, and there is an entry in line 3, it could be a repair business, a commercial art business, or some research activity. If both lines 2 and 3 are blank, it could be a professional or consulting business. If lines 2 and 3 are blank, line 4 also most likely would be blank.

Meaning of "Fabrication Labor"

We have designated line 4 in Figure 6.1 as fabrication labor. On the official tax forms (1040, 1065, and 1120), this line is labeled: Cost of labor. This official phrase is misleading. It implies the cost of all labor, direct and indirect: shop and nonshop. We think that fabrication labor provides a more correct cost connotation.

Our "fabrication labor" is a collective term. It includes all labor associated with the design, manufacture, fabrication, production, processing, finishing, and installing those goods that are — or are intended to be — sold to customers.

Unfortunately, the word "labor" is a tax trap. When you make an entry in line 4 you had better be on your guard. Small businesses are particularly vulnerable.

To the IRS, its agents and computers, the word "labor" means employees. It means persons on your payroll for whom you prepare, annually, those Form W-2s. (Recall Figure 4.4.) If you make any entry in line 4, make sure that the persons you pay are indeed your employees. It's so easy for the Big Computer to cross-check and trap you on this one.

To signal the IRS that you know what you are doing, insert in the white space on line 4 the number of W-2s that you have issued (or will issue). That is, insert the notation "___ W-2s." This tells them that you are not including nonemployees such as outside labor, contract labor, independent contractors, or consultants. The nonemployee labor, if any, is reported on line 5: "other direct costs."

Incidentally, nonfabrication labor comprises office workers, salespersons, warehousing personnel, drivers, owners, and the like. This is indirect-cost labor which goes elsewhere on your federal income tax returns. Do not put these persons on line 4.

Nonemployee Labor: 1099s

We come now to the catchall portion of your direct cost subschedule. This is line 5 in Figure 6.1: *Other direct costs (explain).*

Line 5 consists of five subcategories of other costs. These are:

> (a) Nonemployee labor
> (b) Outside fabricators
> (c) Installation permits
> (d) Freight-in, freight-out
> (e) Other miscellany

Let us devote a few paragraphs to nonemployee labor matters. In small businesses, there is widespread temptation to use nonemployees in order to save paperwork and overhead. We encourage you to do so . . . but with your tax eyes open.

Direct cost nonemployees are those who perform fabrication work, consulting services, specialist tasks, and independent contracting. These are part-time, free-lance workers who are not on your regular payroll. Yet, their personal labor is essential for the goods and services that you provide to customers. Some of these persons are in business for themselves; some are employed elsewhere and are "moonlighting" with you; some are part-time workers needing fill-in work; some are unemployed and will accept any job in the hopes of becoming employed; and some may be family members and friends for whom you are "doing a favor." You engage most of these persons for specific job assignments of a temporary and non-ongoing nature. You have a business to run; you cannot be paternalistic to everybody. The IRS bureaucracy and its revenue agents do not always understand this.

The IRS can be quite ruthless in trying to assert that all nonemployees are indeed your employees. We discussed these matters back in Chapter 4, particularly in Figure 4.1. We are tipping you off here to be on guard.

If you engage nonemployees, there are three things you must do, to deflect IRS attacks.

One. You must have each engagee read and sign a preprinted *Nonemployee Agreement*. This puts the person on notice that he or she is responsible for his/her own income tax and social security tax matters. The agreement also prescribes other understandings. See Figure 6.2 for an outline of points to be included in such an agreement.

Two. You must insist that each engagee submit to you a *Billing Invoice*. Each invoice should contain a brief description of the work performed, the amount charged, and a due date for payment. The invoice(s) should be submitted on a nonperiodic basis, as different phases of the work are completed. If an engagee does not have his own preprinted invoices, direct him to an office supply or stationery store where he can purchase a pad of blank invoices to his liking. The engagee can write or type thereon the billing information needed.

Three. If you pay an engagee the sum of $600 or more in a tax year, you must prepare and submit **Form 1099-MISC**. For this, you need the engagee's social security number. A 1099 is

NONEMPLOYEE AGREEMENT

This AGREEMENT is made between
_____ (called "Principal")
and _____(called "Contractor").

Place of business of Principal:_____
Place of business of Contractor:_____
Work to be performed:_____
_____

End results only. Principal shall exercise no control over Contractor as to manner, means, time, or persons used.

Tools & equipment. Shall be furnished by Contractor at one or more locations as necessary to do the work.

Judgement & discretion. Full right and power of Contractor as he deems necessary to accomplish the work agreed.

Incurrence of liability. Contractor solely liable and responsible for any claims of injury or damage to persons or property.

Available to others. Contractor is free to work for others; however, work above must be completed satisfactorily.

Remuneration by INVOICE. Submission by contractor of itemized billing for each job (or assignment) completed.

Responsible for own taxes. Principal shall not withhold income taxes, social security taxes, unemployment taxes, or any other taxes.

Form 1099 - MISC. Will be issued by Principal upon termination of Agreement or at end of each year, whichever appropriate.

WITNESSED BY	Executed at _____ on _____
_____	_____ /s/ _____ CONTRACTOR Soc. Sec. No.
_____	_____ /s/ _____ PRINCIPAL Fed. I.D.No.
_____	

Fig. 6.2 - Essential Points in a Nonemployee Agreement

comparable, somewhat, to a W-2 — but without the withholdings. An edited version of Form 1099-MISC is presented in Figure 6.3. You have to submit one copy of the 1099 to the IRS, one copy to your state income tax department (if any), and one copy to the engagee. And, of course, you keep one copy for your own records.

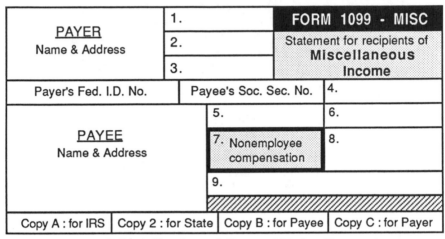

Fig. 6.3 - Edited Version of Form 1099 for Nonemployees

If line 5 (other direct costs) in Figure 6.1 consists of an entry of $600 or more, and you engage one nonemployee or more, we have a "must do" for you. You must — not should — enter in the white space on that line a notation of the number of 1099s issued. Insert the notation "_____ *1099s*." Again, you are putting IRS agents on notice that you know what you are doing. You are also indicating that you have the *payer's copy* on hand to back up your entry. You do keep a copy of each issued 1099-MISC form in your records, don't you?

Every IRS agent is instructed to request that you produce the payer's copy of every 1099-MISC issued. So, be forewarned!

More on "Other Costs"

We listed above five subcategories of other direct costs enterable in line 5 in Figure 6.1. We discussed separately nonemployees (independent contractors) because such is a guaranteed focus of tax attack. Let us now cover the other four subcategories.

Outside fabricators are independent shops and businesses to which you send work for partial processing. They are clearly in business with their own trade name, and with their own billing invoices. They accept work from you along with hundreds of other customers similar to you. They are, in effect, subcontractors to you. There may be certain parts that you want made; there may be special machining, finishing, or testing required; there may be stamping and formation of certain raw materials; or there may be surveying, printing, advertising and other services that you want performed. The point is that you send the work to them, to be processed at their own facilities, with their own equipment, and with their own employees (or nonemployees). Other than for pickup and delivery of the work, or getting assignments, they do not work under your control. When the work is complete, they send you a preprinted invoice and they expect you to pay.

Installation permits are those nuisance fees that you have to pay to local authorities and protection groups for the privilege of sending your workers to customer premises. These costs are most applicable to construction, installation, repair, and demolition activities. The work has to be done on-site (such as remodeling, reroofing, repairing fences, removal of trees, electrical and plumbing installations, and so on). Because of the possible disturbance of neighbors, a separate permit for each job is required.

Freight-in, freight-out are those costs that you pay separately and directly to freight, parcel post, and shipping companies for customer-intended goods and services. If any of these costs are included in those invoices that you receive from your suppliers, or in those invoices that you send to customers, do not enter them on line 5. Otherwise, you would be deducting your freight costs twice.

Other miscellany are those costs that you pay out for "after-sale" settlement activities. For example, your customer has already paid for the work performed and/or goods sold. It later develops that the workmanship is shabby or that the goods malfunction. You have to pay some other person or business (not associated with you) to fix and settle the matter. These costs may include legal and professional fees directly attributable to customer complaints. Any costs related to a specific customer, not included in your regular billing invoices to that customer, are includible on line 5.

If your line 5 entry consists of more than one transactional cost, it is a good idea to attach a separate itemized statement thereto. Enter names, dates, and amounts chronologically. This is what we mean by the word "explain" at line 5 in Figure 6.1.

Line 6 is the subtotal of lines 1 through 5. There's not much explaining to do here.

Importance of Ending Inventory

It is the ending inventory, line 7, that produces the most dramatic effect on your tax status. The higher your ending inventory, the higher your taxes. The lower your ending inventory, the lower your taxes. Sounds weird, doesn't it?

Let us explain. But, first, turn back to Figure 6.1.

For a given subtotal of direct costs (line 6), the higher your ending inventory, the lower your cost of goods and services sold (line 8). For a given amount of gross receipts from your customers, the lower your cost of goods and services, the higher your gross profit. The higher your gross profit — all other expenditures being equal — the higher your tax. It's that simple.

By "juggling" one's ending inventory, one's tax burden can be altered to one's taste. We know this; the IRS knows this; and you probably know this. You can count on the fact that your ending inventory could be — will be — the most tax challenged entry of your direct cost items. It is important, therefore, that you take your ending inventory seriously.

There are eight methods for valuing your ending inventory. Of this number, two are commonly used by small businesses. Method A is the cost method. You simply value your inventory at the end of the year for what you paid for it.

Method B is the "best estimate" method. It consists of checking the inventory on hand either by actual examination or by mental recall, then applying an entrepreneurial "feel" for what it is worth. Method B is not officially sanctioned. Nevertheless, it is frequently used by small businesses. Its weakness is poor documentation for supporting an entry at line 7: ending inventory.

The longer you are in business, the more your ending inventory tends to build up. Old merchandise stays around; exchange merchandise is taken in; new merchandise is bought or produced aggressively with the expectation of expanding the business. The result is that your ending inventory grows and becomes a drag on your cash flow and profit picture.

All ending inventory is tied-up capital. As long as the inventory is on hand, you get no tax benefits for it whatsoever. Even though you may have paid full cash, you get no deduction until it is sold or otherwise disposed. The higher the ending inventory, the higher your bottom-line taxes on income. This exacerbates your desire for, and temptation to, mark down and revalue that inventory.

Ending Valuation Methods

The IRS is alert to your desires and temptations. They recognize only certain valuation methods. Most such methods are designed to keep your ending inventory as high as possible, consistent with real-life business conditions. You are allowed to mark down, but only after your sales history and general economic conditions make it necessary.

Altogether, there are eight officially recognized inventory valuation methods. In a highly abbreviated description of each, we present them all in Figure 6.4. The cost method — called *specific cost identification* — is often the simplest. This is "Method A" mentioned above. But it becomes less and less favorable as your business progresses and market conditions change.

There are too many other valuation methods for us to detail each one here. There are accounting books available which deal strictly with inventory procedures. Just to give you a taste of the procedural detail required, consider the method: *Lower of cost or market value* (Method 3 in Figure 6.4).

To use Method 3, you first have to group and classify all like-kind items. Then, *for each grouping*, you have to document your unit costs and — simultaneously — obtain comparable market value information from "third party" sources. You tabulate all of this information and select the lower figure for each grouping. A highly oversimplified example is as follows:

Item	Cost	Market	Whichever is lower
R	$ 300	$ 500	$ 300
S	200	100	100
T	450	200	200
	$ 950	$ 800	$ 600

Aside from cost-record details, how do you establish market value (as a buyer for resale) on slow-moving, out-of-date, and shopworn items? Answer: You have to obtain written appraisals, clearance sale data, competitor price lists, and used merchandise prices from reliable sources. If you have items which are

METHOD	DESCRIPTION
Your Inventory Choices: Pick One; Stick With It	
1. Specific Cost Identification	Also called "Cost Method". Uses actual invoice cost (less discounts, if any) for each and every item purchased, regardless of when, or in what condition.
2. First-in First-out (FIFO)	Assumes that items purchased or produced first are the ones first sold; cost on invoices for first items purchased/produced used for all items at year end.
3. Lower of Cost or Market	Requires separating all items by category, then tabulating comparable costs and market values; allows selection of lower figure in each category; then all "lower-of" categories summarized.
4. Lower Than Market	Allows mark-down on hard-to-sell, obsolete, and slow-moving items, but only after repeated experience with "special sales" in good faith; promotional inducement costs subtracted.
5. Unsaleable Goods as "Scrap"	Allows use of "scrap value" after demonstrations that certain items or class of items cannot be sold at "distress sale" prices; implies discontinued lines.
6. Perpetual Book Accounting	Requires continuous (daily) record keeping on all purchases/productions <u>and</u> on all sales (at cost); uses "credits minus debits"; very useful when computerized.
7. Manufacturing Full Absorption	Requires listing of all direct production costs <u>plus</u> a prorata allocation of indirect and overhead costs; "prorata" applies to sales and nonsales.
8. Last-in First-out (LIFO)	Assumes that last items purchased or produced are the first items sold; cost on invoices for last items purchased/produced used for all items at year end.

Fig. 6.4 - Recognized Methods for Valuing Ending Inventory

nonsaleable, you have to obtain salvage value data. All of this is tedious and time consuming.

So, too, is the taking of a physical inventory. All eight methods in Figure 6.4 require this. Taking inventory (physically) at the end of each tax year is common practice these days. This practice often generates those well-publicized "inventory sales." Unfortunately, most small businesses tend to guess at their ending inventory rather than physically counting it and valuing it. For tax record purposes, a physical year-end inventory statement, fully itemized, is ideal.

When starting a business, you can choose any inventory method in Figure 6.4 that you want. But once you do so, you have to stick with your chosen method. You cannot change it without getting IRS approval. To get this approval you have to prepare Form 3115: *Application for Change in Accounting Method.* This is a six-page form with approximately 150 questions, statements, checkboxes, and line entries to which you must respond (as applicable).

We repeat again. Once you select an inventory method, you must stick with it. And to make sure that you do, every year on your federal income tax return you will be asked:

Was there any change in determining quantities, costs, or valuations between opening and closing inventory?
☐ *Yes* ☐ *No. If "Yes" attach explanation.*

Putting It All Together

Let us review briefly the essentials of what we have discussed in this chapter. Then let us put them all together and see how they fit into the scheme of things. Keep in mind that we are addressing a major item affecting your federal — and state — income tax: cost of goods and services sold.

Back in Figure 6.1, we listed seven steps for arriving at one's "direct costs" when dealing with customers and clients. For quick summary purposes, we repeat the Figure 6.1 listing as follows:

1. Inventory: beginning of year
2. Purchases for resale
3. Raw materials & supplies
4. Fabrication labor

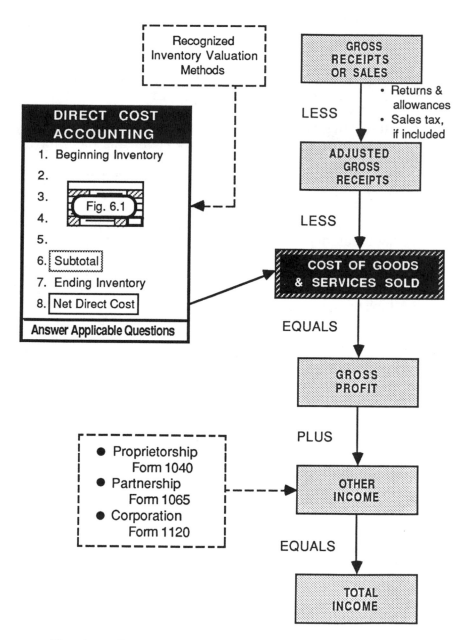

Fig. 6.5 - The Vital Role of Accounting for Direct Costs

5. Other direct costs
6. Subtotal: all of the above
7. Inventory: end of year

When step 7 is subtracted from step 6, we arrive at the net cost of goods and services sold . . . for that tax year.

Figure 6.5 shows you quite clearly how the cost of goods and services sold integrates into your income structure. It directly subtracts from your gross receipts, thereby reducing them for tax purposes down the line.

As discussed, one's ending inventory has a dramatic effect on net cost of goods and services. If the ending inventory is high, your cost of goods is low. This, in turn, increases your gross profits for tax purposes. This means that your direct-cost accounting effort should be focused primarily on the valuation of your ending inventory. If you don't do this, the IRS will.

Just how important each of your direct-cost line entries are (in Figure 6.5) will depend on the nature of your business and your relationships with customers. Another factor is your gross receipts or sales. If your gross receipts are less than $100,000, chances are your cost accounting and bookkeeping practices may not be challenged too rigorously. If your gross receipts exceed $100,000, you'll have to toe the tax accounting line every step of the way.

7

DEFERRED DEDUCTIONS

Not All Expenditures For Business Purposes Are Immediately Tax Deductible In Full. Certain Creative Costs (Usually Intangible) Are Amortized Over 60 Months. Costs Which Enhance The Value Of The Business Or Its Componental Assets Are "Capitalized." They Are Not Recoverable Until The Business Or Assets Are Sold. Tangible Property Items Which Are Purchased And Placed In Service Are Depreciated. Specific Recovery Periods (8 In All) And Depreciation Methods Are Statutorily Prescribed. Depreciation Of "Listed Property" (Involving Personal Use) Is Severely Limited. All Deferred Deductions Are Claimed On Form 4562 (Depreciation And Amortization).

There is one class of deductible expenditures which — sometimes — is hard to explain to first-timers in business. The expenditures that we have in mind are classed as *deferred* deductions. They are "deferred" in the sense that they are stretched out over a period of time. Although fully tax recognized, they are not allowed as an immediate deduction when paid or incurred.

The typical entrepreneurial reaction to deferred deductions is: "If I incur a legitimate expenditure for business purposes, I should get an immediate deduction for it. Why do I have to stretch it out over a period of time? I have to spend my money now. Yet, you tell me that I can't get a corresponding deduction for it! Why not?"

Answer. Certain expenditures are called *capital* expenditures. They are "capital" in the sense that they have *retained value* at the end of the first tax year. They may also have retained value (which diminishes) at the end of the second, third . . . fifth . . . or tenth tax year. Because the acquired items are not fully consumed at the end of the first tax year, the deductions allowable are prorated over a period of years. This is unlike operating expenditures for items and services which are fully consumed within the acquisition year.

The expenditures to which we will be devoting this chapter, therefore, are *amortization*, *capitalization*, and *depreciation*. There are special — and peculiar — tax rules which are applicable. The stretchout and postponement rules are equally applicable to all forms of business, whether proprietorship, partnership, or corporation. A tax understanding of amortization, capitalization, and depreciation is vital to the owner(s) of any business.

What is Amortization?

Amortization is a term which many taxpayers have seen and used, rather automatically. Although frequently used, its tax significance is not always understood.

Amortization is a uniform deduction which applies primarily to the cost of *creating* certain intangibles in a trade or business. The act of creating derives within, by, for, or from each particular business. As such, the created asset is not an item which is ordinarily purchased on the retail market. It is rare that the amortizable costs precede the business to which they apply. Hence, the key distinguishing feature of amortization is creativity . . . rather than purchasability.

In the Introduction to the book, we gave you (perhaps) the best example of the creation of an amortizable asset. This example directed your attention to the startup expenditures of your new business. We told you then that your startup costs were not immediately tax deductible.

As we explained in Chapter 1, startup consists of those intangible costs incurred for the investigation, creation, organizing, consulting, and promoting the idea of a new business. The costs are accumulated — held in suspense — until the business actually gets going. These costs are indigenous to your one business alone. We stressed the accumulation aspects of these costs in Figure 1.4.

There are other examples of the creation of amortizable costs. Among these are organizational and expansion costs, lease and lease modification costs, covenants not to compete, research and development costs, circulation expenditures, market research costs, prepaid insurance contracts, points and fees for business loans, business licenses and franchises, examination and appraisal fees, rehabilitation expenditures, mining exploration and development costs, and many others. All have in common the feature of creativity: one-of-a-kind for each particular business.

Once a business owner has created an amortizable asset, he is allowed — under certain conditions — to take an annual tax deduction against his cumulative costs. To get the deduction, however, four conditions must be met. These conditions are—

One. The amortization deduction must be statutorily allowed. One cannot accumulate costs of choice and amortize them at will.

Two. The amortization deduction must be expressly elected. It is not an automatic deduction as in the case of day-to-day (current) operating expenses. If not expressly elected, it has to be "capitalized." (We'll explain this later.)

Three. The amortization period must be prescribed either by statute or by an enforceable contract. One cannot select a period of his choice. The period must be greater than one year.

Four. The rate of amortization must be uniform and constant (straight line) month to month over the prescribed period. There can be no variation (no acceleration; no deceleration) to match the business income and its cycles.

If a business does not survive the amortization period, the unamortized costs are tax deductible in full, at the time the business ceases. Otherwise, the idea behind amortization is to prorate certain costs over the income-producing life of the business. This proration is designed so that there is no abnormal distortion to net taxable income. This, in principle, is the tax theory.

Items Statutorily Amortized

Amortization is one of those "you can — but you can't" types of deduction that pervade the federal tax laws. You can take the deduction if it is statutorily sanctioned, but you can't take it (even if sanctioned) if you don't elect to do so properly and timely. In the background of every amortization law is the desire by the IRS to disallow the deduction on whatever pretext it can. Your only defense is to cite a specific applicable statute.

There are probably as many as 25 different statutes permitting the amortization deduction. The trouble is, many are buried in subsections of various portions of the tax code, where the word "amortization" is not prominently displayed. Nevertheless, we have dug out 15 amortization laws which we can present to you for illustration purposes. We do this in Figure 7.1.

Obviously, we cannot discuss each and every one of the tax code sections listed in Figure 7.1. Equally obvious, not every section listed is applicable to a small business, especially during its first few years of operation. However, we do want to expand on a few of the sections listed so that you will get the "flavor" of technicalities involved.

Consider, for example, Section 173: Circulation Expenditures. These are costs of market research, advertising, promotion, mailing lists, customer lists, subscription services, and circulation expenses for the publication and distribution of newspapers, magazines, and other periodicals. Section 173(a) says, in part—

> *All expenditures . . . to establish, maintain, or increase the circulation of a newspaper, magazine, or other periodical shall be allowed as a deduction . . . [over a] 3-year amortization period.*

Section 173 obviously applies to large publishers and distributors. But what about small businesses which publish and distribute nonfiction books, advertising brochures, promotional literature, market reports, customer testimonials, newsletters, and the like? There is no specific statute which addresses these items. Our suggestion in a case like this is to use Section 173 as a guide, and amortize the expenditures over a three-year period.

Another section intended for big business but having application to a small business is Section 174: Research and Experimental Expenditures. Section 174(b) thereof reads, in part—

> *At the election of the taxpayer, . . . research or experimental expenditures which are—paid or incurred by a taxpayer in connection with his trade or business . . . may be treated as deferred expenses. In computing taxable income, such deferred expenses shall be allowed as a deduction ratably over such period of not less than 60 months . . . (beginning with the*

month in which the taxpayer first realizes benefits from such expenditures).

INTERNAL REVENUE CODE		
	Amortizable Item	Period
Sec. 169	Pollution Control Facilities	60 months
Sec. 171	Bond (& Indebtedness) Premiums	to maturity
Sec. 173	Circulation Expenditures	3 years
Sec. 174	Research & Experimental Costs	60 months
Sec. 175	Soil & Water Conservation	25% of income
Sec. 177	Trademark & Trade Name Costs	repealed 12/86
Sec. 178	Cost of Aquiring a Lease	term of lease
Sec. 188	Child Care Facilities	repealed 11/90
Sec. 190	Handicapped / Elderly Barrier Removals	$15,000 per year
Sec. 194	Reforestation Expenditures	7 years
Sec. 195	Start-up Expenditures	60 months
Sec. 197	Goodwill & Other Intangibles	15 years
Sec. 248	Corporate Organizational Costs	60 months
Sec. 616	Exploration & Development	10 years
Sec. 709	Partnership Syndication Fees	60 months

Fig. 7.1 - List of Tax Laws Allowing Amortization

As a small business owner, suppose you developed a special computer program for your own business. It takes you several years and a lot of software consulting talent to work out the bugs before you can use the new program in your business. Is this covered by Section 174(b)? Not exactly. But it's close enough. So we suggest using "not less than 60 months" as your amortization period.

As to startup expenditures, Section 195(b) is quite clear. In pertinent part, this section reads—

> *Start-up expenditures may, at the election of the taxpayer, be treated as deferred expenses. Such deferred expenses shall be allowed as a deduction prorated equally over such period of not less than 60 months . . . beginning with the month in which the active trade or business begins.*

If, instead of starting your own business from scratch, you acquire a going business from someone else, the cost of goodwill and certain other intangibles can now be amortized. Prior to 1993, these items had to be capitalized (not treated as deferred expenditures). On point, Section 197 (listed in Figure 7.1) says, in introducing part—

> *A taxpayer shall be entitled to an amortization deduction with respect to any amortizable section 197 intangible . . . ratably over the 15-year period beginning with the month in which such intangible was acquired.*

What is a "Section 197 intangible"? Subsection 197(d) defines it as: (A) goodwill, (B) going concern value, (C) business records and customer lists, (D) licenses and permits, (E) covenants not to compete, and (F) any franchise, trademark, or trade name.

When an amortization rule is repealed (e.g., Sections 177 and 188 in Figure 7.1), the affected expenditures have to be capitalized.

What is Capitalization?

To put it bluntly, the term "capitalization" is a club that the IRS frequently misuses to disallow deductions for alleged *capital expenditures*. A capital expenditure is made when an item or activity created has no ascertainable consumption life. Capital expenditures in business represent tied-up (nondeductible) money until the business is sold, dissolved, or otherwise terminated. At that time, the capital expenditures may be recovered as "return of capital" — which is not taxed.

The classical example of a capital expenditure is land. You pay money to buy a parcel of land to use in your business. Except under extraordinary circumstances, the land cannot be consumed or destroyed. It will be there to the end of your business. You can recover your money then. In the meantime, you get no operating tax deduction for it.

Code Section 263 (Capital Expenditures) makes this point very clear. The introductory part of Section 263 says—

No deduction shall be allowed for—
Any amount paid out for new buildings or for permanent improvements or betterments made to increase the value of any property or estate.

The phrase "betterments made to increase the value of any property" is the tax invocation most often used against businesses to deny them deductions for certain expenditures. For example, the cost of enhancing goodwill, developing an exclusive market niche, or expanding a business are automatically classed as nondeductible capital expenses. Other betterment expenditures which do not fall under a specific amortization statute, also are automatically so classed.   In the real tax world, "capitalization" is the fallback position taken by IRS agents who are unwilling to read or accept the fine print of tax law.

This fallback position was materially strengthened in 1986. Congress then enacted an entirely new section (263A) headed: ***Capitalization and Inclusion in Inventory Costs of Certain Expenses.*** This new section addresses real or tangible property *produced by the taxpayer* and property acquired for resale. Section 263A is now called the "general capitalization rule." It uses the mandatory phrase: *shall be capitalized.*

New regulations expanding on Section 263A have been promulgated. Of particular relevance is Reg. 1.263A-1. It consists of some 35,000 words! This devastating regulation reads in key part—

Except as otherwise provided, all costs that are incurred with respect to real or tangible personal property which is produced, or property which is acquired for resale, are to be capitalized with respect to such property. For purposes of this section, the term "produce" includes construct, build, install, manufacture, develop, improve, create, raise or grow. This section does not apply to:

(1) Property which is not actually used in a trade or business.

(2) Intangible drilling and development costs of oil, gas, or geothermal wells.

(3) Production of property pursuant to a long-term contract.

(4) Research or experimental expenditures covered by Section 174(a).

(5) Timber and certain ornamental trees (raised, harvested, or grown) and the land underlying such trees.

Because of so many words in Section 263A and its regulations, it is virtually impossible to encounter an IRS agent who will read the words intelligently . . . and correctly. They are totally transfixed by the phrase "are to be capitalized." They will not read the exceptions and fine print. They will thus arbitrarily disallow — and capitalize — any expenditure which they don't understand.

Depreciation: Most Understood

In our deferred deductions discourse above, we used a third categorical term: *depreciation*. The depreciation concept is quite well understood by most persons in business (as well as by tax agents). It applies primarily to tangible property items which are purchased for use in business.

The distinguishing feature of depreciation is the *purchase* of property, in contrast to that which is produced or created in one's business. The idea is that property which is purchased and used — "placed in service" as it is called — will be subject to wear and tear, and exhaustion. It will also be subject to obsolescence as new and better property items come into the marketplace. For this wear and tear, a depreciation deduction is allowed.

Section 167 (*Depreciation*) recognizes the deduction allowance quite straightforwardly. Enacted in 1954, the thrust of Section 167 is expressed in its opening paragraph: subsection (a). The first sentence thereof reads in full as—

There shall be allowed as a depreciation deduction a reasonable allowance for the exhaustion, wear and tear (including a reasonable allowance for obsolescence)—

(1) of property used in the trade or business, or
(2) of property held for the production of income.

This reads clearly enough: "There shall be allowed" . . . a depreciation deduction. But what is a "reasonable allowance"? Interpreting this phrase is where taxpayers and tax agents invariably find themselves at odds. To a taxpayer, the phrase "reasonable allowance" means the maximum deduction possible. To a tax agent, it means the minimum deduction possible.

Over the years, Congress has tried to arbitrate the differing interpretive positions of Section 167, particularly subsection (a). But it has not been very successful. It has tried to clarify the issue of reasonableness by adopting the concept of *class lives*. The attempt was embodied in subsection (m) which read, in part, as:

The term "reasonable allowance" as used in subsection (a) means . . . only an allowance based on the class life prescribed by the [IRS] which reasonably reflects the anticipated useful life of that class of property to the industry or other group.

Under subsection 167(m), now repealed, the IRS formulated 15 class lives, ranging from three to 50 years. Still, the IRS insisted that "reasonable" meant the longest class life possible. The longer the class life, the less the depreciation allowance.

Exasperated by the intransigence of the IRS, Congress in 1981 enacted a whole new depreciation section in the tax code. It enacted Section 168: *Accelerated Cost Recovery System.* Evidently, the word "accelerated" was deliberately introduced to counter the IRS's adamant position that "reasonable" always meant the minimum possible depreciation allowance.

Section 168 is a very extensive tax law, which has been amended numerous times since 1981. It is now a complete revision of Section 167.

The "Essence" of Sec. 168

Section 168 significantly clarifies many of the previous controversies surrounding depreciation. Foremost, it throws out IRS's intransigent assertion of "salvage value," which meant that an owner could never recover 100% of his cost. It refines the definition of property classes and recovery periods, yet allows some discretion based on business experience and common sense.

All depreciable property used in an active trade or business is now categorized into **eight** recovery classes. These classes set the recovery periods (in years) over which the acquisition cost of the items in each class is 100% recovered. At the end of each recovery class period, if the property is still in service, there is no cost value left. Thereafter, the depreciation deductions cease altogether.

The eight recovery classes are prescribed in Section 168(e): *Classification of Property*. This section reads in part as—

Property shall be classified under the following table:

Class No.	Property shall be treated as:	If such property has a class life (in years) of:
1.	3-year property	4 or less
2.	5-year property	More than 4 but less than 10
3.	7-year property	10 or more but less than 16
4.	10-year property	16 or more but less than 20
5.	15-year property	20 or more but less than 25
6.	20-year property	25 or more
7.	Residential rental	27.5 [straight line]
8.	Nonresidential realty	39 [straight line]

Examples of the kinds of items depreciable in each of Classes 1 through 6 are presented in Figure 7.2. Classes 7 and 8 are rather self-explanatory. They have very long recovery periods (and low rates of depreciation) which may not be of pressing interest to new businesses getting started. It is also doubtful that small businesses would be significantly involved in Classes 5 and 6.

All property in Classes 1 through 6 must use the *half-year convention* (Sec. 168(d)(1)). This is a presumption that all property placed in service (or disposed of) during the taxable year took place on July 1st of that year. This means that in the first (or last) year of service, the maximum depreciation deduction possible is six months. This is so, even if property is placed in service on January 1st or taken out of service on December 31st. The half-year convention is intended to encourage business owners to place and remove depreciable items more or less uniformly throughout the year, rather than bunching them up into one time frame for tax reasons.

To discourage bunching up at year end, a special mid-quarter rule applies: Sec. 168(d)(3). This rule triggers in when more than

Class	Recovery Period	Useful Life	Examples Only [Not all Inclusive]
	CLASSIFICATION OF PROPERTY : SECTION 168 (e)		
1	3 years	4 or less years	Small tools; Jigs & dies; Computer software; Handling devices (baskets, carts, pallets, trays); Race horses over 2 years old.
2	5 years	4 to 10 years	Autos & light trucks; Computers & peripherals (non-main frame); Light manufacturing equipment; Telephones; R&D items; Office equipment; Medical equipment.
3	7 years	10 to 16 years	Furniture & fixtures; Heavy-duty vehicles (tractors); Storage structures (agricultural, horticultural); Large tools & machinery; Railroad track;Trailers; Drilling equipment.
4	10 years	16 to 20 years	Railroad tank cars; Marine shipping containers; Manufactured homes (mobile); Theme structures (signs); Utility lines & equipment; Heavy duty shop machinery; Main frame computers; Pollution control equipment.
5	15 years	20 to 25 years	Production & treatment plants (water, sewerage, steam,gas, electricity, oil); 2-way communication systems; Irrigation systems; Food processing plants.
6	20 years	over 25 years	Locomotives; Ships; Airplanes; Recreational vehicles (pleasure boats); Municipal systems (docks, airfields, hangars); Roadways, bridges, fences; Resource recovery plants; Amusement & entertainment facilities (instruments & equipment).

Fig. 7.2 - Example Depreciable Items in Each Recovery Period

40% of all depreciable items for the year are placed in service during the last three months of the year. When this happens, all property is treated as having been placed in service at the mid-quarter of each calendar quarter in which it is first used. This adds undue complication to your depreciation scheduling. The obvious way out is to avoid placing 40% or more items in service during the months of October, November, and December.

MACRS Depreciation Methods

There is a new buzzword in depreciation circles these days. It is MACRS (M-A-C-R-S). This is an acronym for Modified Accelerated Cost Recovery System. When Section 168 was first enacted in 1981, the acronym then used was ACRS (Accelerated Cost Recovery System) was enacted as Section 168. ACRS prescribed only four enticingly short recovery periods: 3-, 5-, 10-, and 15-year. In 1986, these recovery periods were "modified" — meaning: substantially extended to the eight periods tabulated above. In short, MACRS is ACRS made less attractive.

Whereas ACRS prescribed a separate depreciation method for each of its four recovery classes, MACRS limits the depreciation methods to two (for Classes 1 through 6). These two methods are:

> 200% declining balance (for Classes 1 through 4)
> 150% declining balance (for Classes 5 and 6)

The MACRS statutory wording now reads—

Sec. 168(a) — *The depreciation deduction provided by section 167(a)* [pre-1981 law] *for any tangible property shall be determined by using—*
(1) the applicable depreciation method,
(2) the applicable recovery period, and
(3) the applicable convention.

Sec. 168(b) — *The applicable depreciation method is—*

(1) [For 3-, 5-, 7-, and 10-year property]
(A) the 200 percent declining balance method,
(B) switching to the straight line method for the 1st taxable year for which using the

straight line method with respect to the adjusted basis as of the beginning of such year will yield a larger allowance.

(2) [For 15- and 20-year property]
(A) the 150 percent declining balance method,
(B) switching to straight line [as above].

The "switching" to straight line is necessary in order to achieve 100% recovery at the end of each recovery period. Without switching, the declining balance method leaves some unrecovered basis at the end of each period.

Let us illustrate the switching necessity with a numerical example. Consider an item of 5-year property costing $10,000 and placed in service in a new business. The comparative depreciation deductions are as follows:

	200% Declining	Straight line	Switched
1st year (6 mo)	2,000	1,000	2,000
2nd year	3,200	2,000	3,200
3rd year	1,920	2,000	2,000
4th year	1,152	2,000	2,000
5th year	691	2,000	800
Subtotals	8,963	9,000	10,000
6th year (6 mo)	207	1,000	---
Totals	9,170	10,000	10,000

Caution: In order to achieve full recovery in the switched mode, the property must remain in service for the full 12 months of the final year. This means that removal from service (if any) cannot take place until the first month of the following year. (This is the 6th year in the example above.)

There is an alternative to the switching mode. As per subsection 168(g)(1)(E), one can always elect to use the *straight line method* from the first year on (called: "Alternate Depreciation System"). Doing so permits a more uniform month-to-month depreciation allowance by using the "mid-month" convention of subsection 168(d)(4)(B). Small businesses, particularly, will find straight line depreciation simpler during their trial-and-error years of getting started.

Special Depreciation Election: Sec. 179

Businesses, especially new/small businesses, need to recover their capital outlays for depreciable assets as rapidly as possible. Otherwise, much needed money is tied up for long periods of time. When tied up, the money cannot be used in the business to keep it operating and keep it solvent.   Congress was receptive to this concern when it enacted Section 179: *Election to Expense Certain Depreciable Business Assets.*

The idea behind Section 179 is to permit small businesses to get an immediate upfront writeoff (deduction) for selected depreciable expenditures.   Here, the term "small business" pertains to the purchase of depreciable items totalling less than $200,000.   The maximum upfront deduction is $25,000 (phased in) for each taxable year that Section 179 property is placed in service.   "Section 179 property" is defined as *any recovery property* (Section 168) of a tangible nature which is acquired by purchase for use in the active conduct of one's trade or business.

For your familiarization purposes, selected excerpts from Section 179 are as follows:

Subsec. (a)   —   *A taxpayer may elect to treat the cost of any section 179 property as an expense which is not chargeable to capital account. Any cost so treated shall be allowed as a deduction for the year in which the property is placed in service.*

Subsec. (b)   —   *The aggregate cost which may be taken into account under subsection (a) for any taxable year shall not exceed . . . the applicable amount* [$17,500 for 1996; $18,000 for 1997; $18,500 for 1998; $19,000 for 1999; $20,000 for 2000; $24,000 for 2001, 2002; $25,000 for 2003 or thereafter].

Subsec. (c)   —   *An election under this section for any taxable year shall . . . be made on the taxpayer's return . . . in such manner as the* [IRS] *may by regulations prescribe.*

The regulations prescribe that the election be made on Form 4562: Depreciation and Amortization. It is made by appropriate entries in the columnar portions of Form 4562 titled: "Election to Expense Certain Tangible Property."

Column (a) — *Description of property.* This is a short description of the property for which you make the election, together with a notation of its class life (3-yr, 5-yr, 10-yr).

Column (b) — *Date placed in service.* This is the date of the property's first active use in the business: **not** its date of purchase. The property can be bought in one year, but not actively used until one or more years later.

Column (c) — *Cost.* This is the full purchase (list) price of the item or items, without any adjustment to cost for items (if any) that you traded in.

Column (d) — *Elected cost.* This means the amount of cost that you choose to expense. You may choose to expense only part of the cost, and depreciate the rest of it.

Once you have made the Section 179 election, it becomes irrevocable (Sec. 179(c)(2)). That is, you cannot change your mind after the due date for filing your return. The purpose of this is to prevent you from "playing games" with the depreciation system. Depreciation is an ongoing year-to-year accounting affair.

Introduction to Form 4562

The official heading on Form 4562 is *Depreciation and Amortization.* It consists of six parts, namely: Part I (Sec. 179 Election), Part II (MACRS Depreciation), Part III (Other Depreciation), Part IV (Summary), Part V (Listed Property), and Part VI (Amortization). Parts I through IV appear on page 1; Parts V and VI appear on page 2 (the reverse side of page 1).

The general format and content of Form 4562 (pages 1 and 2) is presented in Figure 7.3. We have edited this form quite extensively, to help you get a better sense of its purpose. It is primarily a current-year summary form. Deductions for prior-year property and expenditures must be scheduled separately on backup attachments.

A headnote on Form 4562 says: *See separate instructions.* These instructions consist of approximately 10,000 words! There is no way that every business taxpayer is going to read every word of these official instructions. Furthermore, the instructions refer you to other IRS forms and publications. Unfortunately, by not reading the official instructions you may wind up underpaying or

Form 4562	DEPRECIATION AND AMORTIZATION	Tax Year

Part I — Election to Expense Certain Tangible Property

- ■ Statutory limit
- ■ Taxable Income limit
- ■ Total elected cost
- ■ Carryover of unused

Note: If you have "Listed Property", Complete Part V

Part II — MACRS Depreciation: Current Year

- ☐ 8 property classes
- ☐ Business use basics
- ☐ 7 columnar entries
- ☐ Method/convention

Do Not Include Listed Property

Part III — Other Depreciation: Prior Years(s)

- ■ From Worksheet 4562W
- ■ Pre MACRS
- ■ Prior MACRS
- ■ Improvements

Do Not Include Listed Property

Part IV — Summary: Enter on "Appropriate Lines" of Return

- ☐ Listed property (p.2)
- ☐ Nonpersonal items

Part V — Listed Property - Autos, Phones, Computers, etc.

Section A: Depreciation Deduction
- ■ 9 columnar entries
- ■ Over 50% BUP

Section B: Information Regarding Use of Vehicles
- ☐ 4 mileage questions   ☐ 3 other questions ☐ 6 vehicles

Section C: Questions for Employers
- ■ 5 questions
- ■ Company cars
- ■ Employee personal uses

Part VI — Amortization (of Capitalized Expenditures)

- ☐ Current Amortization
- ☐ Prior Amortization
- ☐ 6 columnar entries
- ☐ Specific code sections

Enter on "Other Expenses/Deductions" Line

Fig. 7.3 - Abridged Format/Contents of Form 4562

overpaying your proper tax. All depreciation rules have an impact on the profitability or unprofitability of new business.

A forewarning to Part I says—

Use Part V for automobiles, certain other vehicles, cellular telephones, computers, and property used for entertainment, recreation, or amusement.

Thus, right away, certain items — called "listed property" — are excluded from Part I: Election to Expense (Sec. 179). Listed property has extensive personal/pleasure-use implications. This means that more stringent rules apply. After you apply these rules in Part V, you can enter the qualified Section 179 portion in Part I.

We have already discussed the $17,500/$25,000 election feature of Part I. The only additional point that you need be aware of is that you can exercise the election only for the **more than 50%** business-use portion of listed property in Part V. We'll have more to say on Part V later.

Part II of Form 4562 is where most of the nonlisted property action is. It applies only to property placed in service during the *current year*. This portion of the form recapitulates the eight "recovery classes" of MACRS property that we outlined earlier. The entry columnar headings are:

(a) Classification of property
(b) Month and year placed in service
(c) Basis for depreciation (business-use only)
(d) Recovery period
(e) Convention
(f) Method
(g) Depreciation deduction

You show all of your computations directly on this form. If you placed MACRS property in service in prior years, you have to keep track of it separately and cumulatively.

Part III of Form 4562 permits you to use any other-than-MACRS allowable method of deprciation that you prefer. However, there are no explicit columnar entries as in Part II. This means that you have to develop your own format for substantiating the single-line entries in Part III.

Part VI (Amortization) of Form 4562 provides for columnar entries in a fairly straight-forward manner. Description of the property (Column (a)) and its applicable code section (Column (d)) can be ascertained from Figure 7.1. Again, only current-year property is shown; you need separate documentation on prior-year property.

Overall, there is one major drawback to Form 4562. It is designed for current-year deductions only. There is no provision for recording the extension of computations for prior year expenditures. The official instructions on this point say—

The basis and amounts claimed for depreciation [and amortization] *in prior years should be part of your permanent books and records.*

This is a warning that you prepare backup substantiation for each of the prior-year line entries on Form 4562.

Part V of Form 4562 (Listed Property)

Listed property (autos, computers, cellulars, recreationals, etc.) is a very sensitive tax matter. Computing the proper depreciation allowed takes up most of the space on page 2 of Form 4562. The Part V portion is divided into three sections, namely:

> Section A — Depreciation (Automobiles, Computers, and Other Listed Property)
> Section B — Information Regarding Use of Vehicles
> Section C — Questions for Employers Providing Vehicles to Employees.

Part V is devoted exclusively to items which have a high probability for substantial personal use. Its entire thrust is ferreting out the personal use aspects of alleged business uses of property. This ferreting starts right at the beginning of Section A, where you are asked:

> *Do you have evidence to support the business use claimed?*
> ☐ *Yes* ☐ *No*
> *If "Yes," is the evidence written?* ☐ *Yes* ☐ *No*

Listed property rules are prescribed in Section 280F. These were enacted in 1984 with the primary focus on expensive (luxury) passenger autos used in business. A "luxury" auto is one costing more than $15,000. Other items are luxurious if used in business 50% or less of the time. Much attention in Section 280F is devoted to your establishing the *qualified business use* of items that go on Part V (280F(d)(6)).

In Section B of Part V, for example, the following questions are asked pertaining to vehicles:

1. Total business miles driven   _____
2. Total commuting miles driven   _____
3. Total other (noncommuting) miles driven   _____
4. Total miles driven during the year   _____
5. Was the vehicle available for personal use during off-duty hours?   ☐ Yes ☐ No
6. Is another vehicle available for personal use?   ☐ Yes ☐ No

The purpose of these and other questions and checkboxes on Part V is to force you to think, document, and write down specific numbers. You must establish quantitatively your true *business use percentage* (BUP). Estimates and guesstimates are no longer acceptable. Your BUP — whatever it turns out to be — has to be expressly entered in a separate column of its own (in Section A). If your BUP is 50% or less, other limitation rules are triggered.

If, as an employer, you allow company-owned vehicles to be used by your employees, you must answer five more questions. The first one is—

Do you maintain a written policy statement that prohibits all personal use of vehicles, including commuting, by your employees? ☐ *Yes* ☐ *No*.

. . . And on and on.

The purpose of the Yes-No checkboxes above is to alert you to the importance of written evidence. In the case of a passenger automobile, this means a *business mileage log*. If there is more than one vehicle being used for business, a separate mileage log for each must be kept.

Virtually every passenger vehicle is capable of carrying one or more persons who are not engaged in business. This fact alone is justification for the IRS to assert that such a vehicle is used 100% for personal purposes and 0% for business. To counter this stance, you must be able to produce a mileage log showing each business destination and its round trip mileage. If there is more than one business destination on a given day, you may aggregate the mileage for that day. If certain business destinations are repeated throughout the year, each may be separately coded and mileaged (at the front or back of the diary). Then only the code symbol need be entered for each proper day. If you indeed go to the effort of keeping an updated business mileage log on each highway vehicle, it (the diary) will work wonders when your car and truck expenses are tax challenged.

As you can probably appreciate by now, Part V of Form 4562 requires extreme documentary detail. You can make yourself a slave to this effort, if you want to. But our suggestion is that you eliminate entirely all personal usage of depreciable items claimed in business. With the exception of passenger vehicles, a "no personal use" policy can be mandated for computers, office equipment, entertainment facilities, and recreational items.

8

FORM 1040 PROPRIETORSHIPS

> For Proprietorships, Schedule C (1040) Is
> Where All The Action Is. This Is Your Basic
> Profit Or Loss Statement On Which Some 25
> Official Deduction Categories Are Preprinted.
> There Are Other Forms Associated With
> Schedule C, The Most Important Being Form
> 4562 (Depreciation And Amortization) And
> Schedule SE (Self-Employment Tax). In The
> Head Portion of Schedule C There Are Certain
> Questions And Check-Boxes That Must Be
> Answered. If You Claim Office-At-Home
> And/Or Car And Truck Expenses, Your
> "Business Use Percentage" Must Be
> Established. Travel, Meals, And Entertain-
> ment Require Extreme Documentary Detail.

In this chapter, we want to focus exclusively on proprietorships. This is the simplest form of business, and illustrates the basic accounting involvement of any trade or business. Whether you operate as a proprietorship or not, the material in this chapter is a tax prelude to that for partnerships and corporations.

We have in mind two particular areas for discussion. One area is the gamut of tax forms involved. These differ substantially for each form of business. We are not going to fill out the forms; we are just going to tell you which ones are applicable — and why. We will go into some detail, however, into the central (basic) form required. For proprietorships, this is Schedule C (Form 1040).

Our second area for discussion has to do with selected fully deductible current expenses. We will pick three of these which are highly vulnerable to tax challenge. For proprietorships, these are: (1) office-in-home, (2) car and truck expenses, and (3) travel and entertainment. We will pick other current expenses for in-depth discussion when we get to partnerships and corporations. We also will touch on cash-vs-accrual method of tax accounting, so that you will at least understand the difference.

We will stick solely with proprietorship activities. We will not get into other sources of income that you might have, as these require separate tax forms of their own. Nor will we repeat the discussions in previous chapters. So as to limit our scope, we will avoid any discussion of pension, profit-sharing, or other retirement plans. Don't worry; we will discuss retirement plans in Chapter 11 (Compensation of Owners).

Overview of Forms Required

The existence of Form 1040: U.S. Individual Income Tax Return, is well known. Every individual (married or single) earning income of any kind — from business or otherwise — files this form. The front page of this form is arranged into approximately 15 lines for reporting specific sources of income. Of these 15 lines, only one pertains to the reporting of proprietorship income.

The one proprietorship line reads, officially, as follows:

Business income or (loss) (attach Schedule C)

The intended entry, of course, is the *net* profit or loss; not the gross. The intention of this line entry would be more self-explanatory if the official wording were "Proprietorship net profit or (loss)." The attachment of Schedule C does make this more clear.

For proprietorships, therefore, the basic tax form is **Schedule C (Form 1040)**. Its official heading is—

Profit or Loss From Business
(Sole Proprietorship)
▶ *Attach to Form 1040*   ▶ *See Instructions*

The very first line entry on Schedule C is *Name of proprietor* (singular). It does not say proprietors (plural). This is important to note. Many husbands and wives in business together think of themselves both as the proprietors of the same business. And, indeed, they may well be. But only one can be named on Schedule C as the sole proprietor. There is a reason for this. It has to do with the self-employment tax (Schedule SE) which is a separate tax on each proprietor. We'll discuss Schedule SE separately later.

For the same husband and wife business, it is possible to file two Schedule C's: one "his"; one "hers." The two Schedule C's must be treated as separate businesses, each with its own separate books of account. The instructions on this point say—

If you had more than one business, or if you and your spouse had separate businesses, you must complete a Schedule C for each business.

In other words, there is no prohibition against attaching multiple Schedule C's to the same Form 1040.

Before we get into other Schedule C details, we should give you a quick overview of all the tax forms associated with Schedule C. We do this in Figure 8.1. Please take a moment and glance at it.

Those form numbers shown in bold in Figure 8.1 are specifically mentioned on Schedule C itself. If they apply, you MUST attach them. There are three of such forms, namely: 4562, 8829, and 6198. This is the order in which they appear on Schedule C. There also are three "other related" forms. These related forms are mentioned, as applicable, in the instructions to Schedule C.

Form 4562 (in Figure 8.1) is the depreciation and amortization form we discussed in Chapter 7 (Deferred Deductions). Almost every proprietorship claims depreciation expense in one manner or another.

Form 8829 is officially titled: Expenses for Business Use of Your Home. Many startup proprietorships use the personal residence of the proprietor as the principal place of business, at least initially. It is economical to do so. However, there are stringent rules for figuring the amount of expense deduction that you are allowed. Form 8829 steps you through these rules in a sequential and methodical manner.

As to **Form 6198** (At-Risk Limitations), Schedule C carries this notice—

If you have a loss, you MUST check the box that describes your investment in this activity:
    ☐ *All investment is at risk.*

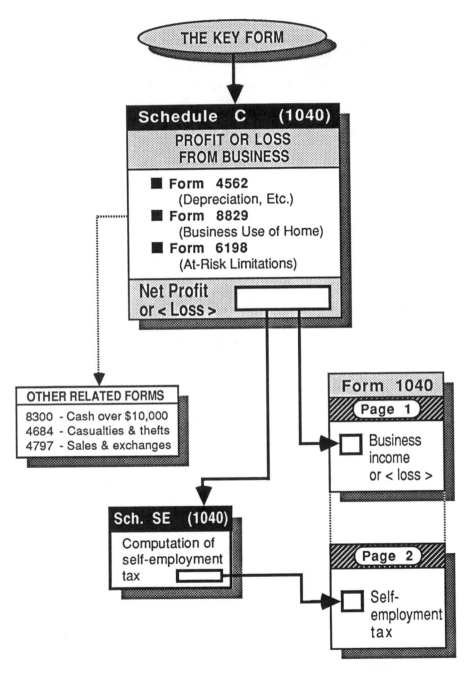

Fig. 8.1 - Tax Forms Associated with a Proprietorship

☐ *Some investment is not at risk.*

The phrase "not at risk" means operating your business with borrowed money (loans) which are nonrecourse (unsecured), protected by stop-loss guarantees, or informal advances from family members and/or close business associates. There is nothing tax-wrong with borrowing money to use in your business, so long as you have a legal (enforceable) obligation to pay it back. If you have such obligation, Form 6198 does not apply. Obviously, we are recommending that you position yourself to check the "All" box.

Other Related Forms

In Figure 8.1, there is reference to three other tax forms. These forms, and their official headings are:

Form 8300 — Report of Cash Payments Over $10,000 Received in a Trade or Business

Form 4684 — Casualties and Thefts to Property Used in a Trade or Business

Form 4797 — Gains and Losses From Sales or Exchanges of Assets Used in a Trade or Business and Involuntary Conversions

These forms are applicable to partnerships and corporations, as well as to proprietorships. Each form says, "Attach to your tax return" (1040, 1065, 1120). A few words on each is instructive.

If you receive from a customer, client, or other person (or organization) cash of more than $10,000 in one or more related transactions, you may be required to prepare Form 8300. We say "may be required" because much depends on the nature of the cash received, from whom, for what purpose, and under what circumstances. Form 8300 requires you to detail all of this, including the actual count of the number of $100 bills received.

You do **not** attach Form 8300 to Schedule C. Instead, within 15 days after the cash transaction, you file it with the IRS in Detroit.

For Form 8300 purposes, "cash" is defined as coin (gold or silver), U.S. currency, and foreign currency. It is that which is customarily used as *bearer money*. It is that which is accepted on its face value: no signatures required; no guarantees required; no personal references required. The $10,000 count is that which takes place in a 24-hour period with the same person. So, if someone brings large amounts of cash to you, start your clock before you rush off to prepare Form 8300. If it looks like the cash bearer is going to approach the $10,000 figure, direct him to a local bank. Instruct him to bring back to you a cashier's check instead. Cashier's checks, regardless of the amount — could be $1,000,000 or more — do not have to be reported on Form 8300. We think you have more important things to do than being an informant for the IRS on your cash customers.

Form 4684 (Casualties and Thefts) is in two parts. Section A is for personal use property; Section B is for business use property. In either case, you have to describe each property item that is damaged, destroyed, or stolen. You have to take into account the amount of insurance reimbursement, if any. You have to get a professional appraisal of the property "before and after" the casualty, and then you have to compute its change in fair market value. If your insurance reimbursement is greater than the loss in value, you have net taxable income rather than a tax recognized loss.

Form 4684 and the casualty/theft rules therewith are quite complex. Whatever the outcome, the information is not entered on Schedule C. It is entered on Form 4797 and then subsequently onto Form 1040.

Form 4797 is a very complicated form, far beyond the scope of our discussion here. We could devote a whole chapter to this one form alone. Its primary use is when a business is sold, exchanged, bankrupt, or involuntarily converted (by condemnation or threat thereof). It is also useful when the major assets of a business are being disposed of. In these situations, you are dealing in *capital* transactions (capital gains and/or capital losses). These are not the ordinary profit or loss activities of a startup and ongoing business. The information from Form 4797 goes to other schedules on your return, but not on Schedule C.

Format/Content of Schedule C

Schedule C (Form 1040) is *the* tax form of concern to every proprietor: whether in a trade, business, or profession. Unless you are in a partnership, corporation, or are a full-time employee to someone else in business, Schedule C is the form for you. It is a basic profit-or-loss statement that is useful for other purposes besides tax return filings. You should master this form.

Schedule C (Form 1040)	PROFIT OR (LOSS) : PROPRIETORSHIP	Tax Year

Name	Soc. Sec. No.
Principal business	Business Code
Business address	Employer I.D.

General Information

Accounting method ☐ Cash ☐ Accrual ☐ Other
Inventory method ☐ Cost ☐ Lower ☐ Other

	Yes	No
● Any change in closing inventory ?		
● Did you "materially participate" ?		
● Any deduction for office-at-home ?		
● File all employer quarterly returns ?		
● Still in business at end of year ?		

Part I Income

Gross receipts or sales . . . . _____
● _____   _____
● _____   _____
● _____   _____
● _____   _____

Your total income > > > > > > > > > > > > > > [   ]

Part II Deductions

(See Fig. 8.3)   (See Fig. 8.4)

Other expenses (specify)
. . . . _____
. . . . _____
. . . . _____

Total deductions ⟶ [   ]

NET PROFIT OR (LOSS) ⟶ [   ]

Fig. 8.2 - General Format / Content of Schedule C (1040)

Without the officialese, we present in Figure 8.2 our edited version of Schedule C. We want you to become familiar with its general format and content, and not with every official line entry thereon. The official forms and line numbers change from year to year. We are showing page 1 only, as that is where all of the P or L action is.

In Figure 8.2, we first call your attention to the second line there. The full official wording on that line is—

Principal business or profession, including product or service. Principal business code.

In the instructions to Schedule C is a listing of approximately 175 business activities which the IRS has computer coded. Each activity is assigned a separate 4-digit code. You are told to—

Select the activity code that identifies (or most closely identifies) the business or profession that is the principal source of your sales and receipts.

Obviously, the purpose of this codification is to make it easier for the IRS to computer-match and track your business activities.

Overall, Schedule C consists of the following parts:

Page 1	Page 2	
General Information	Part III	— Cost of Goods Sold
Part I — Income	Part IV	— Information on Vehicles
Part II — Expenses	Part V	— Other Expenses

We have covered Parts I and III sufficiently back in Chapter 6 (Cost of Goods Sold). In fact, Part III is almost exactly the same subschedule presented in Figure 6.1. So, there is no point repeating these matters here. We have tried in Figure 8.2 to focus attention on the head portion (general information) and on Part II (expenses). As you will note, Part II is detailed in Figures 8.3 and 8.4.

The head portion consists of about a dozen informational statements, questions, and checkboxes, such as: *Do you "materially participate" in the operation of this business?* ☐ *Yes* ☐ *No.* These

Sequence	ITEM		Amount
	Schedule C : Deduction Categories		
001	Advertising	(printing & promotions)	
002	Bad debts	(accrual method only)	
003	Bank charges	(include credit cards)	
004	Car & truck expenses	(business only)	
005	Commissions	(paid to others)	
006	Depletion	(resource extraction)	
007	Depreciation	(from Form 4562)	
008	Dues & pubs.	(seminars & newsletters)	
009	Employee benefits	(food, prizes, & awards)	
010	Freight out	(postage & parcel post)	
011	Insurance	(business only)	
012	Interest: Mortgage	(on real property)	
013	Interest: Other	(on business loans)	
014	Laundry & cleaning	(include uniforms)	
015	Legal & professional	(consultants)	
016	Office expense	(stationery & other)	
017	Pension plans	(for employees only)	
018	Rent	(paid on business property)	
019	Repairs	(painting & maintenance)	
020	Supplies	(small tools & materials)	
021	Taxes	(payroll, property, licenses)	
022	Travel & lodging	(documented)	
023	Meals & entertainment	(less 20% for yourself)	
024	Phone & utilities	(business only)	
025	Wages	(gross amount: nonshop)	
026 to 030	Other expenses	(SPECIFY)	

Fig. 8.3 - Preprinted Deduction Lines on Schedule C (1040)

items are designed to test your tax knowledge and expertise. If applicable, make sure you answer correctly.

In Part II, there are approximately 25 official expense deduction lines. We have taken liberty in Figure 8.3 to amplify and redesignate the lines into a 3-digit sequence of numbers. We also have added some short explanatory wording. We have done this so that you might use the digit sequencing for coding into your own system of accounts. The proper coding of allowable (current expense) deductions is crucial to your tax survival. If you are careless or sloppy in these matters, you *will* pay a price. You will not get the expense deductions that you think you are entitled to.

Cash vs Accrual Accounting

In the head portion of Schedule C, there is a 3-checkbox line which reads:

Accounting method: ☐ *Cash* ☐ *Accrual* ☐ *Other (specify)*

If you check *Other*, you could enter the word "hybrid." This could be a combination of cash and accrual. The question arises: What is the distinction between cash and accrual methods of accounting?

In the first place, the term "cash" as a method of accounting is not limited to coin and currency. It includes all forms of payment receipts: checks, credit card charges, negotiable instruments, property, services, barter, debt relief, and other. Whenever you enter a payment credit to an income producing account, you have received cash. For example, you invoice a customer for $1,635. He/she gives you a check for $800, with the understanding that the balance will be paid later. Your cash-basis income for that transaction is $800.

The same rationale applies, in reverse, when you owe someone money. For example, a retailer, after processing your order for office supplies, submits an invoice to you for $1,485. You pay $500 on the account, with the promise to pay the balance later. Your cash-basis deduction for that transaction is $500.

Thus, if you had just the one income transaction above, and the one expenditure transaction — in a given taxable year — your profit would be $300 ($800 income less $500 expense).

In contrast, the accrual method of accounting says your profit is $150 ($1,635 income less $1,485 expense). On the accrual basis, when you invoice a customer, that's income ($1,635 in the example above). When a supplier invoices you, that's a deductible expense ($1,485 in the example above).

Regulation 1.446-1(c)(1)(ii) describes accrual accounting as—

Generally, under an accrual method, income is to be included for the taxable year when all the events have occurred which fix the right to receive such income and the amount thereof can be determined with reasonable accuracy. Under such a method, deductions are allowable for the taxable year in which all the events have occurred which establish the fact of the liability giving rise to such deduction and the amount thereof can be determined with reasonable accuracy.

This regulation follows from Section 446 of the tax code. This section says that any acceptable method can be used, so long as it clearly reflects income, and is consistently used from year to year. Once you select a method, you cannot change to another method without written authorization from the IRS (via Form 3115).

Another regulation (Reg. 1.446-1(c)(2)(i) says—

In any case in which it is necessary to use an inventory, the accrual method of accounting must be used with regard to purchases and sales unless otherwise authorized.

The point here is that if your business consists primarily of inventory (purchased, processed, or manufactured) being sold, you have to use the accrual method. However, if inventory sales represent less than 50% of your business, you can use the cash/accrual hybrid. If you use the hybrid method, you must use the accrual method with respect to purchases and sales (of inventory) and you may use the cash method for all other items of income and expense (Reg. 1.446-1(c)(1)(iv)).

Office-at-Home Deduction

Near the bottom of Schedule C (on page 1), there is a line entry that reads—

*Expenses for business use of your home. Attach **Form 8829**.*

We want to tell you about the office-at-home deduction.

Many proprietorship businesses do have an office at home. This helps to cut down overhead. But more importantly, proprietorship businesses usually require an owner's attention 12 to 16 hours a day. One needs the privacy and quiet of his home to do his thinking, planning, worrying, and posting his books of account. An office at home is also useful for seeing clients, interviewing employees, discussions with sales/advertising staff, storing valuable inventory, and conducting other business transactions which are impractical to conduct in the open marketplace.

In any bona fide business, expenses associated with an office are fully deductible. With an office at home, however, the implication is that it is used for personal purposes as well. Because of this implication, special rules have been enacted (Sec. 280A) to deny certain expense deductions when there is an operating loss from the business.

Section 280A of the tax code is titled: **Disallowance of Certain Expenses in Connection with Business Use of Home.** This section is a general prohibition against claiming office-at-home expenses. It is targeted primarily at employees (engineers, teachers, salespersons, programmers) and part-time entrepreneurs in hobbies, sports, recreational activities, investments, and direct sales. Indirectly, it raises the question: What is your primary income-producing activity? If so engaged for primary income, the expenses are allowed.

Subsection 280A(c)(1) says that the general disallowance rule—

shall not apply to any item to the extent such item is allocable to a portion of the dwelling unit which is exclusively used on a regular basis—
*(A) as the **principal place** for any trade or business of the taxpayer, [or]*
*(B) as a **place of business** which is used by patients, clients, or customers in meeting or dealing with the taxpayer in the normal course of his trade or business.*
The term "principal place" includes [that] which is used . . . for administrative or management activities . . . if there is no other fixed location of such trade or business.

The phrase "portion of the dwelling unit" means the business use portion or percentage (BUP). The BUP is determined by taking square footage measurements of the office space (including walls, access, and storage), and dividing this figure by the total living space (square footage) of the residence. A diagrammatic sketch of the office-at-home arrangement, with all dimensions thereon, becomes an important tax document.

There is also another requirement: "exclusive use" on a "regular basis." In other words, your office-at-home must have all the earmarks and similarities to a regular business office that you could have rented in a commercial complex. It has to be unsuitable for personal and family living. Once you have met this requirement, you are entitled — proportionately — to such deductible expenses as:

property taxes	telephone
mortgage interest	all utilities
hazard insurance	office supplies
painting & repairs	office equipment
cleaning & maintenance	carpets & drapes
depreciation	furniture & fixtures

That is, you are entitled to these expenses so long as you keep separate business records on them. You must go out of your way to avoid any commingling of these expenses with your personal living expenditures.

Car & Truck Expenses

Many proprietors have at least two vehicles that are used for business purposes. They have a passenger auto and a light truck or van. They may have other vehicles, but these two are typical. The car is used for calling on customers and suppliers, seminar attendance, appearance at government offices, and so on. The truck or van is used for pickup of supplies purchased and for delivery of products sold, for carrying tools and parts, for installation and repair services, and for the display of samples and catalogs.

Here, again, we run into the implication of personal and family use. To a tax agent, any use of a car or truck in a proprietorship business is deemed to be personally used, unless proven otherwise. This means that unless a BUP (business use percentage) is convincingly established, no expense for operating the vehicle is allowed.

In the case of a passenger auto, the BUP proof requires maintaining a very detailed *mileage log*. We acquainted you with the mileage questions asked in Part V of Form 4562, in the latter part of Chapter 7. There is no use trying to rationalize or argue that your passenger auto is 100% used in business. It may well be. Even if you have a separate car for your personal use, and a separate car for the personal use of each of your family members, the IRS simply will not take your word for it. They want to see a mileage log showing dates, places, distances, and business purpose. If you have your office at home and a place of business elsewhere, you are commuting from home to work. This is nonbusiness use.

The situation is different with a truck or van that is fitted out for your particular business. If it has special racks, shelves, tie-down bars and hooks, and other modifications for hauling supplies, inventory, tools, and displays, you may be able to convince a tax agent that, indeed, you have a 100% business vehicle. This is especially convincing if you have a very uncomfortable nondriver's seat, and the vehicle is not suitable for weekend camping. To establish this, you should have complete photographs of the vehicle.

With proper attention to your business use needs, your truck or van may qualify as a *nonpersonal use vehicle*. This means a vehicle which, by reason of its nature, is not likely to be used more than a de minimis amount for personal purposes. If this is so, there is no mileage log requirement (Sec. 274(i) and Sec. 280F(d)(5)(B)(iii)).

Once you have met the mileage log requirements for a passenger auto and the "qualified nonpersonal use" requirements for a truck or van, you are entitled to the following expense deductions:

gas & oil	license fees
tires & batteries	parking & tolls
repairs	garaging costs
maintenance	car washes
insurance	installed items
interest payments	rental payments

Obviously, you must have records to substantiate the car and truck expenses that you enter on Schedule C.

Travel, Meals, & Entertainment

There is one tax subject that we are quite reluctant to touch on. It is a very sensitive expenditure category called TME (Travel, Meals, & Entertainment). Tax agents fancifully imagine that every struggling proprietorship is living high on the hog — wining and dining and living gloriously — at government expense. As a result of this unrestrained imagination by the IRS, new tough tax rules enacted in 1986 severely limit all TME expense deductions.

The IRS regulations on TME expenditures would fill this entire book. The key reference on point is Regulation 1.274: *Disallowance of Certain Entertainment, Gift, Travel, and Meal Expenses*. It consists of approximately 30,000 words. Yes: 30,000 words! If you prefer a shorter version, Code Section 274 (Disallowance of Certain Entertainment, Etc., Expenses) consists of approximately 5,000 words.

Altogether, there are approximately 35,000 words of tax law and regulations on TME expenditures. These are independent of special revenue rulings, court decisions, and arbitrary interpretations by overzealous tax agents. We simply cannot cover TME adequately in the space allotted in this chapter. We just want you to be aware of the difficulties involved.

The term "travel" for tax purposes means *away from home overnight* . . . on a bona fide business trip. It includes transportation and lodging only. The term "meals" means any food or beverage, which is not lavish or extravagant, consumed when the taxpayer on business is present. The term "entertainment" means gifts and social affairs (theater, sport events, banquets, dancing) which has a clear business purposes.

Needless to say, every item of TME expenses must be documented in detail: Who, What, When, Where, and Why. Yet, even with the most painstaking records, only 50% of the meals and entertainment are deductible.

On Schedule C, your TME gets special treatment. There is a separate subschedule thereon which requires four line entries. We have enlarged and presented this subschedule in Figure 8.4. Any entry on a TME line over $100 is guaranteed to be a picky-picky issue by the IRS. In the IRS's eyes, any TME expense entry is an abhorrent act by a taxpayer.

Other Expenses (Specify)

If you glance at Figures 8.2, 8.3, and 8.4 for a moment, you will note that the last deduction entry line is "Other expenses." You are instructed to specify these expenses in Part V. This means that you must identify, reference, and list the amount of each such expense. You cannot insert "miscellaneous" and enter whatever amount you want. For Schedule C purposes, there is no such thing as a miscellaneous expense.

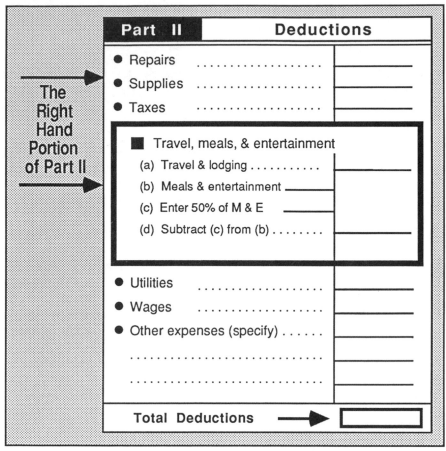

Fig. 8.4 - The TME Subschedule on Schedule C (1040)

The official Schedule C form lists approximately 25 current expense categories. If you incur other types of business expenses which are not officially listed, you may enter them, as appropriate, in the "Other expenses" category. There are nine lines in Part V (on page 2) for this purpose. Each line space is about six inches long. This implies that you are expected to make each entry as self-explanatory as possible. Above all, avoid using the term "miscellaneous."

All types of business expense deductions come under the general tax code Section 162: *Trade or Business Expenses.* The opening sentence reads in full as—

There shall be allowed as a deduction all the ordinary and necessary expenses paid or incurred during the taxable year in carrying on any trade or business.

This section is more commonly referred to as the "ordinary and necessary" (O&N) rule. Hence, if you have an O&N expense which is not line categorized on Schedule C, you enter it on the other expense line.

What are some examples of "other expenses"?

For one, Amortization. (Recall Figure 7.3, Form 4562, Part VI.) There is no categorical line for this on Schedule C. So, enter it in the first blank space under other expenses as—

Amortization: Form 4562 .... $_____

Another example, suppose you incurred some research and experimental expenditures in connection with your business. This is a Section 174(a) deduction. You enter on the next blank space—

Sec. 174(a) expense .... $_____

A third example could be educational expenses for maintaining or improving your skills as an entrepreneur or specialist. A situation like this is covered by Regulation 1.162-5(c). On Schedule C, do not use the phrase "educational expenses"; it has prebusiness connotations. Instead, use "professional development" and enter on the third blank space—

Prof. develop. Reg. 1.162-5(c).............. $_____

We are trying to stress an important point with these three examples. You give a short (acceptable sounding) description of the expense, and immediately follow it with a specific reference. The reference may be a tax form number, a tax code section, or a tax regulation number. For other allowable expenses, you may reference a Revenue Ruling or Tax Court decision. By citing specific references, you are putting the IRS on notice that you know what you are doing. You want the expense deduction as claimed.

Suppose you have some doubt(s) about the clear deductibility of an expense item? So long as it qualifies in your mind as O&N, try to "force fit" it into the nearest applicable categorical line on Schedule C. This assumes, of course, that you have proper backup documentation. There is no point in calling attention to a questionable expense by entering it into separate blank spaces at the end of your Schedule C.

Schedule SE: The "Second" Tax

The very last line entry on Schedule C is: *Net profit or (loss).* Assuming there is a net profit, there are *two* taxes that are imposed on this amount. There is the regular income tax. There is also a *self-employment* (SE) tax. In many cases, the SE tax is greater than the regular income tax. This is because there are no offsets or adjustments to the SE tax, as in the case of income tax.

The first tax is computed by entering the net profit from Schedule C onto page 1 of Form 1040 (as per Figure 8.1). There it combines with other sources of income to arrive at one's total (gross) income. From this gross, certain adjustments are subtracted, for example, your retirement plan contributions. This gives an adjusted gross income (AGI). From the AGI, itemized personal deductions are subtracted, then your personal exemptions are subtracted. This gives a taxable income to which the regular tax rates apply. This is your first tax. It appears in the upper portion of page 2 of Form 1040.

The second tax is computed by entering the same net profit above onto Schedule SE (Form 1040). The official heading of this schedule is: *Self-Employment Tax.* This schedule steps you through the computations for arriving at your Social Security tax AND your Medicare tax. The two rates differ. Currently, the Social Security tax rate is 12.4% of your net Schedule C earnings . . . up to *around* $65,000 . . . and increasing. The Medicare tax rate is 2.9% of your net earnings up to infinity. The two tax computations combine to become your SE (self-employment) tax.

In addition to your Schedule C net earnings, you may have self-employment income from a partnership, and/or from non-Schedule C activities (such as consulting fees, author royalties, incidental commissions). All are combined and treated as self-employment income for the SE tax. For purposes of this tax, a self-employed person is taxed both as an employer *and* as an employee.

In 1985, the maximum SE tax assessable was just under $5,000. By year 2000, the maximum may well exceed $20,000. This second income tax is no trivial matter.

9

FORM 1065 PARTNERSHIPS

A Partnership Is Not A Taxable Entity. As Such, Its Form 1065 Is An "Information" Return: Not A Tax Return. It Consists Of Income Sources, Allowable Deductions, Cost Of Goods, Balance Sheets, And Data On The Participation Of Partners. The 1065 Information Is Distributively Allocated And "Passed Through" To Each Partner. Ideally, The Partnership Accounting Year Should End On September 30. This Allows 90 Days Before Each Partner Closes His Tax Books On December 31. Each Partner's "Distributive Share" Is Itemized On A Schedule K-1 (1065) Which Directs Attention To Specific Tax Forms That Each Partner Must Use.

In this chapter we address partnerships, their tax forms, and their peculiarities of tax treatment. As you will soon see, a partnership return is significantly more complex than a proprietorship return. Part of this is due to the fact that more than one owner is involved. Although many of the profit/loss elements are the same, there are other elements in a partnership return which are not present in a proprietorship.

The basic partnership return is Form 1065. This form is officially titled: **U.S. Partnership Return of Income.** Compare this with Form 1040 which is titled: U.S. Individual Income Tax Return. Note the titling difference. The partnership form uses the phrase "Return of Income," whereas the proprietorship form uses "Income Tax Return." What is missing in the Form 1065 title?

The word "**tax**" does not appear.

A partnership, in and of itself, is not a taxable entity. Yes: a tax accountable income or loss is determined. Whatever the amount is, it is passed through — proportionately — to the individual partners for taxing on each of their own separate Form 1040's. There is no tax computation whatsoever on a partnership return. More appropriately, then, a partnership 1065 is an *information* return, rather than a tax return.

A partnership can consist of any two or more persons (3, 5, 10) who join together to carry on a trade or business. If there are too many persons involved, matters can get overly complex. This is because the tax information from Form 1065 has to be equitably reconciled, before being passed through to each partner.

Since this is an instructional guide, we want to avoid unnecessary complications. For our purposes, therefore, we will treat all partnerships as consisting of three unrelated persons, each of whom is a "material participant" in the new business. They work together for livelihood purposes, rather than for tax shelter benefits. This is the essence of a general partnership which we explained back in Chapter 2.

The Partnership Accounting Year

One of the first acts of reconciliation is for the partners-to-be to adopt an allowable accounting year for the partnership. This is important because the partnership is an entity separate and apart from the individual partners themselves. As a separate accounting entity, a separate set of books is required. Posting, maintaining, and summarizing the accounts at a specific year-end date is absolutely essential to the success of the partnership.

For a newly formed partnership, the general rule is that the partnership year must end . . .*within or with the taxable year of the partner*(s) [Sec. 706(a)]. Most individual partners are on a calendar year basis. It is a rare exception to be otherwise. Hence, the phrase "within or with" means before or on December 31 of each year.

If, in a three-member partnership, the partnership year also ends on December 31, that becomes four tax returns to be simultaneously reconciled. This is the seedbed for making mistakes and for causing arguments and disharmony between partners. Tax return preparation is an acid test of self-discipline and resolve. Not all

Form 1040 filers function with the same degree of conscientiousness. Now you know why we are limiting our discussion to three-person partnerships.

To avoid the December 31 accounting panic, we urge adopting a partnership year ending on September 30. This is the end of a calendar quarter: the 3rd quarter. A calendar quarter accounting year coincides nicely with employer quarterly returns and quarterly sales/use tax returns. A September 30 partnership year precedes each partner's calendar year by 90 days. This should be ample time to get the partnership books in order, and pass the results on through to the individual partners.

Unfortunately, the partners cannot arbitrarily adopt a September 30 partnership year on their own. They must obtain IRS approval. This requires filing Form 1128 (Application to Adopt, Change, or Retain a Tax Year) and stating the reasons for wanting September 30. Section 706(b)(1)(c) authorizes the IRS to insist on a *business purpose* for any date other than December 31.

If the nature of the partnership business is such that there is a "natural business year," you have a legitimate reason for change. Most businesses have natural peaks and nonpeak periods. For some businesses, there is an optimum period for the introduction of new models, new products, and new services. If you have such a natural business year, do claim it. (Recall Fig. 1.5.)

In most cases, the IRS will approve Form 1128 if the partnership date requested is not earlier than September 30 or not later than December 31. Other than this 90-day "window," approval for other partnership accounting years can be obtained. But it is difficult. The partnership has to have at least three years of prior operating experience in order to deviate from the September 30-December 31 window.

Written Partnership Agreement

A partnership is an unincorporated combination of persons of legal age who agree, formally or informally — orally or in writing — to conduct a business jointly. There must be a mutual intent and desire to so join. There also must be a mutual desire to actually conduct a valid business for profit-seeking purposes. Each partner thereto must devote his "best efforts" towards achieving the partnership goal. In addition, each partner must contribute either money, property, or services (or a combination thereof).

If one contributes money, property, and/or services to a business venture, some common sense should prevail. Foremost in this regard is that the partnership agreement be in writing. It need not be a formal document in high-sounding legalese. Just something in writing, logically organized, and in words and phrases that all partners understand. All partners should read and sign the agreement in the presence of at least one witness, preferably a Notary Public. Does this not make good sense?

All partnerships have one bad feature. They start falling apart when the first ill winds of business blow. In the euphoria of creation, everyone agrees amicably to share in the profits. Everyone also has an obligation to share in the losses and setbacks. If a squeamish partner starts turning away, you want a contractual document to hold his feet to the fire. In short, you want a legally enforceable contract. This means that the partnership agreement must be in writing and signed by all parties concerned. Do not commit your money, property, or time until you have a meaningful partnership agreement in hand.

For federal tax purposes, a valid partnership must have five requisites. These are:

1. There must be a partnership agreement . . . in writing.
2. The parties must have represented to each other that they are partners (for tax information sharing).
3. Each partner must have a proprietorship interest in the profits *and* an obligation to share in the losses.
4. The parties must have a right to control the conduct of the business, including access to the books thereof and the disbursement of income therefrom.
5. Each party must have contributed either capital, property, or services.

While profit or loss sharing is a requisite of any partnership, the profits or losses need not be shared in exact proportion to the value of each partner's contributed capital, property, or services. So long as the nonproportionate sharing is spelled out in the partnership agreement, the IRS generally will accept the agreed-to allocations. There is only one condition that the IRS imposes on nonproportionate sharing. That is, the economic reasoning for the nonproportionate sharing must be sound, and it must be independent of any tax consequences to the individual partners.

Some of the introductory points of a sound but simple partnership agreement are presented in Figure 9.1. Some partnership agreements can run 10 to 15 pages long. This is much too long. It is impossible to cover every possible and unforeseen contingency. Three pages covering the high points is enough. Do note, particularly, in Figure 9.1 that a *managing partner* is designated. This is the person responsible for all record keeping and tax accounting for the partnership.

A partnership is presumed to be ongoing and continuing from year to year, unless it is terminated. Section 708(b) spells out when termination occurs. In part, this tax code section reads—

A partnership shall be considered as terminated only if—
   (A)   no part of any business, financial operation, or venture of the partnership continues to be carried on by any of its partners . . . or,
   (B)   within a 12-month period there is a sale or exchange of 50 percent or more of the total interest in the partnership capital and profits.

Although it is not necessary to put this termination rule in the partnership agreement, it is a good idea to do so. It may save misunderstandings when a more than 50% partner (or partners) withdraws from the activity.

Each Partner's Capital Account

One of the first accounting tasks for the managing partner is to set up a separate capital account for each partner. This can be done on a single ledger with separate columns assigned to each partner. The capital accounts are used for determining each partner's proportionate ownership interest in the partnership, and for allocating his distributive share items at the end of each partnership year.

If each partner contributed money only — and nothing else — each partner's beginning capital account would be quite simple. Money in cash or check is denoted in dollars. Thus, the capital account of each of three partners would be—

Partner A	—	X dollars
Partner B	—	Y dollars
Partner C	—	Z dollars

PARTNERSHIP AGREEMENT

This AGREEMENT is made between
_____ , (called Partner "A")
_____ , (called Partner "B")
and _____ , (called Partner "C")

These parties voluntarily associate themselves together as General Partners for the purpose of conducting the business of _____
_____ .

Name & Duration.   The name of the partnership shall be
_____. The partnership shall continue until dissolved by mutual consent or as otherwise terminated.

Place of Business.   The principal place of business shall be
_____ and such other place or places as may be mutually agreed upon.

Initial Capital.   The initial capital of the partnership shall be $ _____ , and each partner shall contribute as follows:
        Partner "A" $_____ (or the equivalent)
        Partner "B" $_____ (or the equivalent)
        Partner "C" $_____ (or the equivalent)

Books of Account.   The partnership shall keep accurate, up-to-date, and complete books of account at all times. Said books shall be open to examination by any partner.

Managing Partner.   The partners mutually agree that
_____ (Partner "A") shall act as managing partner to prepare the books of account, all tax returns, and all other documents pertaining to the business .

WITNESSED BY	Executed at _____ on _____
_____	_____ , Partner "A"
_____	_____ , Partner "B"
(Notary Public)	_____ , Partner "C"

Fig. 9.1 - Introductory Points in a Partnership Agreement

Most active partnerships, however, are formed largely with property and services being contributed. There is some money contributed but, often, the amount is less than 50% of the initial capitalization of the venture. Property is contributed in the form of real estate, machinery and equipment, materials and supplies, inventory, accounts receivable, securities, installment notes, and so on. Services are contributed in the form of past services rendered, special expertise and know-how, and guaranteed immediate services.

All nonmonetary contributions have to be fair market valued at the time of their acceptance by the partnership. Written appraisals and other estimates and documentation are needed to back up the dollar value assigned to each contributor. Special rules apply (Sec. 724) for unrealized receivables, inventory items, and capital loss property. When all property and services are fair valued, they are treated thereafter as ordinary capital.

Each partner's capital account has a "beginning of year" and an "end of year" amount. In between these two amounts, various changes take place. There may be additional capital contributions or capital withdrawals. There are allocations of ordinary income or loss, capital gain or loss, nontaxable income, unallowable losses, and other internal accounting adjustments (for loans, bad debts, credits).

A sample capital account ledger for a three-person partnership is presented in Figure 9.2. For each entry line, there is a separate account for each partner, and a summary total for all partners. Entry lines (d) and (e) particularly should be noted. These are transactional items which do not show up directly in the income/loss accounting on the partnership return. They are separate distributive share pass-throughs.

There is one other line entry to note in Figure 9.2. It is line (h): *partner-days*. In some business ventures, the number of partners comes and goes. They "buy in" and "sell out" on short notice. When they do, the partnership mix is changed from that of the initial formation. To properly allocate the distributive share items, the capital-active number of days of each partner in the partnership year should be recorded.

Quick Overview of Form 1065

The partnership Form 1065 is significantly more complex than the proprietorship Schedule C (Form 1040). There are several

CAPITAL ITEM		Partner "A"	Partner "B"	Partner "C"	TOTAL (All Partners)
(a)	Beginning of year				
(b)	Contributed during year				
(c)	Ordinary income (loss)				
(d)	Income not in (c)	{ Capital gain & return / Nontaxable interest / Other (see instructions)			
(e)	Losses not in (c)	{ Capital losses / Nondeductible expenses / Other (see instructions)			
(f)	Withdrawals & distributions				
(g)	End of year				
(h)	Partner days				Schedule M Form 1065

Fig. 9.2 - Capital Account Ledger for Each Individual Partner

reasons for this. The principal reason is that in a partnership there are more owners and more capital available to engage in a multiplicity of ventures, simultaneously. There are portfolio income and expenses, rental real estate income and expenses, capital gains and losses, and investments in other partnerships and businesses. There is also a balance sheet requirement for identifying the assets and liabilities of the partnership.

With these preliminary comments in mind, it is instructive to present a quick overview of the format/content of Form 1065. We do this in Figure 9.3. Note that we show two "spread sheets"; but actually, Form 1065 consists of *four* full pages. We have taken much liberty to simplify Form 1065 for our purposes.

At the top of page 1 of Form 1065, there are separate entry spaces for date business started, and for total assets at end of year.

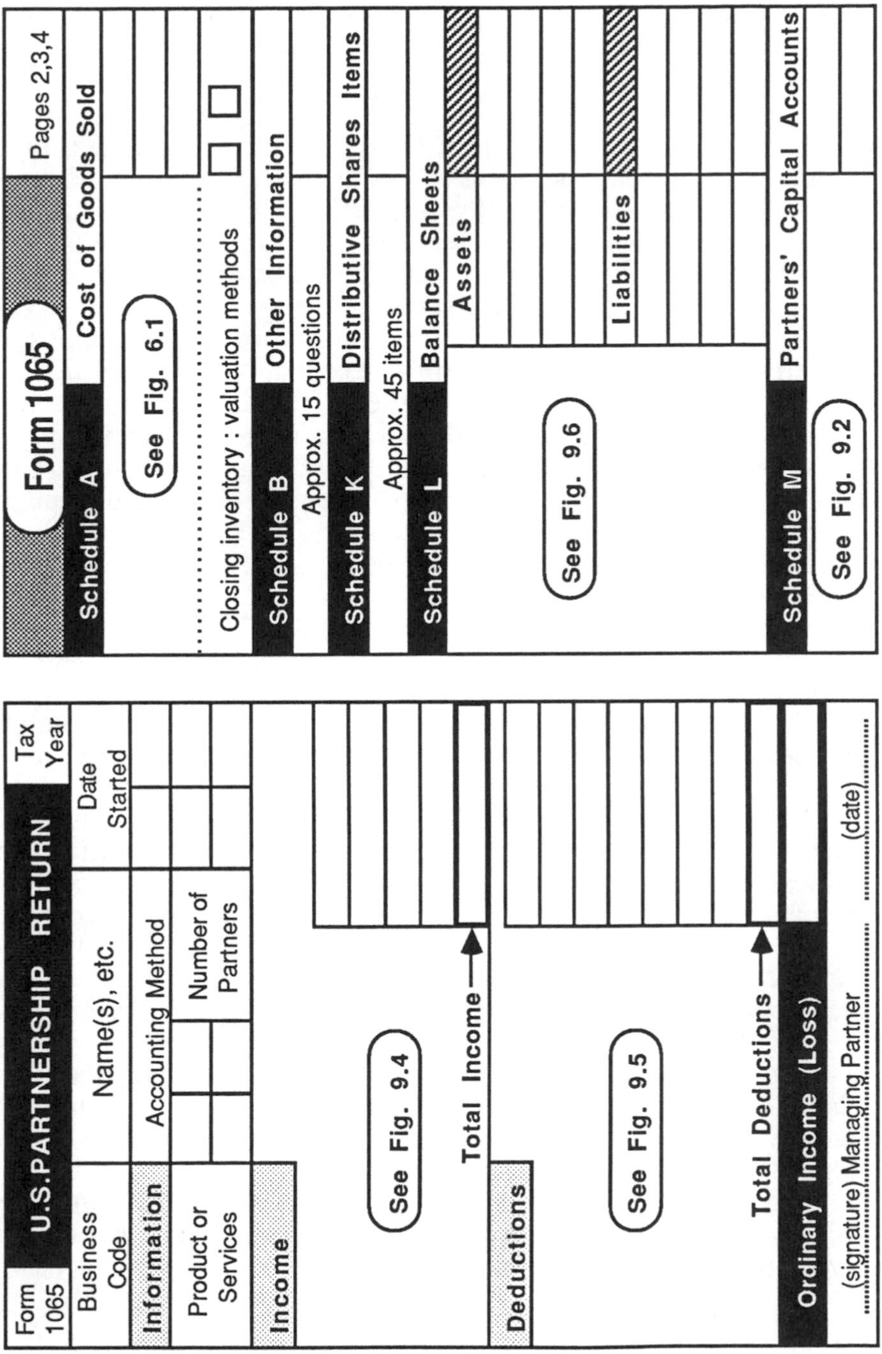

Fig. 9.3 - Oversimplified Format / Contents of Partnership Return

There also are a number of check-boxes which focus on the type of return, method of accounting, and number of partners in the partnership.

The income and deductions portions of page 1 are comparable — somewhat — to the profit or loss format/content of a proprietorship. But more items and more segregations are required. The bottom line on Form 1065 is officially designated *Ordinary income (loss)* rather than net profit or loss. This is because there is no netting until the partnership pass-throughs are combined with each partner's other sources of income.

Pages 2, 3, and 4 of Form 1065 consist of five schedules as identified in Figure 9.3. **Schedule A** (Cost of Goods Sold) has been covered previously in Chapter 6 (Fig. 6.1). There are a few more questions on the valuing of closing inventory, especially with regard to "subnormal" goods and "full absorption" of manufacturing costs. Partnerships tend to be suspect of tax gamesmanship, and so more questions and check-boxes are used.

Schedule B (Other Information) asks some 12 to 15 questions in Yes-No check-box form. These focus on the type of partnership, whether other partnerships are involved, and whether there are any foreign partners. Questions are also asked whether the partnership is publicly traded, whether it is a tax shelter, and whether there are any foreign bank accounts. If there were any distributions from the partnership by sale or death during the year, an attached statement is required showing basis adjustments to the remaining partners.

Schedule K (Distributive Share Items) lists approximately 45 different items of income, credits, and deductions which are allocated to each partner individually. For this allocation, an associated Schedule **K-1** (1065) is required. More on the contents of this K-1 later.

Schedule L (Balance Sheets) consists of some 20 asset and liability entry lines. Schedule L is required when the gross receipts *and* total assets of the partnership exceed $250,000.

We already have introduced to you **Schedule M** (Partners' Capital Accounts). We did this, in a different format, in Figure 9.2. Below Schedule M, there is separate space for "Designation of Tax Matters Partner" (the Managing Partner).

We meant it when we said a "quick overview" of Form 1065. We just wanted to introductively familiarize you with it. As you can sense, it is not an ordinary profit or loss statement.

Multiple Sources of Income

Unlike a proprietorship which focuses primarily on one trade or business, with some incidental other income source, a partnership can conduct several primary businesses simultaneously. Much depends on the individual expertise of the individual partners. Usually, there is one primary (central) business in which all partners materially participate. Then there are one or more satellite businesses, each overseen and managed by a separate partner. There can be rental income property, participation in a farming or mining venture, affiliation with another partnership, investments in mutual funds, and so on. Indeed, for truly active partnerships, multiple sources of income tend to be the rule rather than the exception.

To accommodate the multiplicity of income sources, the income summary portion of Form 1065 has to be expanded significantly. For each separate income source, a separate backup schedule is needed. This is for tracking purposes. All income into the partnership is not treated the same when passed through to the individual partners. For example, material participation income is subject to social security tax, whereas rental income, capital gain income, and interest/dividend income are not subject to said tax. Certain items such as rental income and portfolio income are subject to passive loss and interest expense limitation rules. Tracing all income sources, therefore, becomes particularly important in partnerships.

In Figure 9.4 we present an edited and rearranged version of the income portion of Form 1065 (page 1). Note that lines 1 through 5 represent the "core business" of the partnership; lines 6 through 14 are the "satellite" businesses.

We are not going to describe each of the income sources in Figure 9.4. Most are self-explanatory and are particularly so when the backup schedules are used. As a point of interest, however, you might want to compare Figure 9.4 with Figure 6.5 (in Chapter 6). Both are near-identical down to gross profit. It is the box labeled "other income" in Figure 6.5 where the partnership differences commence.

Deductions Sequence Rearranged

All businesses are entitled to certain current expense deductions. We presented a rather extensive list of these deductions (for

STARTING YOUR BUSINESS

Page 1	PARTNERSHIP INCOME	TAX YEAR
No.	ITEM	Amount
1	Gross receipts or sales	
2	LESS returns & allowances	
3	Balance (adjusted gross receipts)	
4	Cost of goods sold	
5	Gross profit (subtract line 4 from line 3)	
6	Income (loss) from other partnerships	
7	Income (loss) from fiduciaries	
8	Portfolio income (loss)	
9	Rental realty income (loss)	
10	Other rental income (loss) [Equip. rental]	
11	Net royalty income (loss) [Oil & gas]	
12	Net farm income (loss) [Sch. F (1040)]	
13	Net Form 4797 gain (loss) [Asset sales]	
14	Other income (loss) [Attach Sched.]	
	TOTAL INCOME ⟶	

Fig. 9.4 - Rearranged Income Lines on Form 1065

proprietorships) in Figures 8.3 and 8.4. Similar deductions apply to a partnership. The difference is the sequence of arrangement. Certain deductions are prioritized in a partnership for pass-through reasons and for highlighting terms of the partnership agreement.

For example, guaranteed payments to a partner or partners. Guaranteed payments are of two kinds: (1) compensation for services rendered, and (2) interest on separate money loaned to the partnership.

A partner, as such, is not an employee of his partnership. This is because he is a part owner of the business and shares directly in its net profits. If he is to be assigned any compensation for his services, the assignment must be specifically set forth in the partnership agreement. If it is so, then his compensation is a "guaranteed payment." It is deductible from the partnership income.

A partner also is a venture capitalist. He has to advance (contribute) money to the partnership to get it started and keep it going. Ordinarily, a partner is not expected to lend money to his own partnership. He may do so, however, if sanctioned by the partnership agreement. Any loan by a partner to the partnership must be backed up with a promissory note signed by the partners, with the market rate of interest stated thereon. With this documentation, the interest paid to the partner is a guaranteed payment of the partnership, and deductible by it.

With the foregoing in mind, the sequence of deductions against the income of a partnership is presented in Figure 9.5. Do note the second deduction entry: Salaries and wages. These are *other than* any guaranteed payments to the partners, and other than direct labor

Page 1	INCOME Fig. 9.4	TAX YEAR
	PARTNERSHIP DEDUCTIONS	
No.	ITEM	Amount
1	Guaranteed payments (to partners)	
2	Salaries & wages (not to partners)	
3	Rent paid (for buildings, equip., etc.)	
4	Deductible interest (core business only)	
5	Taxes, licenses, & permits	
6	Bad debts (accrual only)	
7	Repairs (to business property)	
8	Depreciation (from Form 4562)	
9	Amortization (from Form 4562)	
10	Retirement plans (employees only)	
11	Employee benefit programs	
12	Other deductions (attach schedule)	
	TOTAL DEDUCTIONS ⟶	

Fig. 9.5 - Rearranged Deduction Lines on Form 1065

in the cost-of-goods-sold schedule (Sch. A of Fig. 9.3). This deduction comprises the usual administrative salaries and wages paid to employees of the partnership.

Also note the third deduction in Figure 9.5: Rent paid. Because a partnership has to have a central place of business, the renting of commercial office or shop space is quite typical. The location should coincide with the business address in the partnership agreement. If also sanctioned in the agreement, the partnership may rent tools, machinery, equipment, furniture, and fixtures. All rents paid for the business use of property is deductible. This does *not* include car rentals of any kind. Special disallowance rules apply to passenger vehicles valued at more than $15,000 (Sec. 280F).

If a partnership borrows money from one or more financial institutions for its core business, the interest on that money is deductible by the partnership. However, virtually all other forms of interest expense (particularly for the satellite businesses) are subject to limitations, capitalizations, and phase-outs. Hence, it is very important to read the official instructions on what interest is deductible by the partnership.

Altogether there are approximately 12 preprinted deduction lines on Form 1065. This compares with approximately 25 for a proprietorship (Fig. 8.3). The unlisted deductions on Form 1065 are all combined in the last entry: *Other deductions (attach schedule)*. Make absolutely sure that none of these other deductions includes any personal expenditures of the partners, nor any losses on self-dealing transactions between the partners and the partnership.

Importance of Balance Sheets

Very few partnerships are all-liquid: with nothing but cash money on hand or in the bank. There are certain tangible and intangible assets which are carried on the books from year to year. And there are certain legal obligations which remain to be paid.

All assets and all liabilities of the partnership at the end of each accounting year are set forth on *balance sheets*. The plural "s" derives from the fact that there is a balance sheet for the beginning of the year, and another balance sheet at the end of the year. When placed side by side, the two balance sheets give a concise picture of the comparative results for that year.

Technically, the posting of balance sheets is not required unless the gross receipts *and* total assets of the partnership exceed

$250,000. But, as a partner, you want the information posted regardless of any tax requirement. This posting should be mandated in the partnership agreement. There is no better way of determining the "net worth" of a business than the posting of balance sheets. If done correctly, the net worth should exactly equal the combined capital accounts of all the partners. Hence, the balance sheets are a means for cross-checking and reconciling the *capital accounting* practices of the partnership.

Our edited version of the balance sheets for a partnership are presented in Figure 9.6. Actually, the categories listed, and the sequence shown, follow very closely the official format of Form 1065. We have tried to make the itemizations a little more self-explanatory. The "beginning of year" balance sheet is the "end of year" data from the preceding year.

Note in Figure 9.6 that the accounts receivable are reduced by the uncollectible accounts at the end of the year. Uncollectibles are those customer billings which are more than 90 days past due and for which a "final demand" in writing has been made. If there is no response of any kind within 30 days of the final demand, you might as well write the amounts off. Legal action for collection can be costly and is often ineffectual. Every partner should know the uncollectibles (bad debt) experience of his partnership.

The asset entries for depreciation, depletion, and amortization require subtractions of the accumulated deductions previously taken. This includes the current year's deduction as well. The net depreciation, net depletion, and net amortization is the "book value" of these assets at the end of the year. Unless there is real estate involved, it is unlikely that any of these assets will appreciate in value with time. Hence, book value is a realistic tool for ascertaining the net worth of a business.

The assets and liabilities of a business both are valued in terms of time. Accounts which are due and payable within one year are classed as "current" items. Those which are due and payable in one year or more are classed as "long term." Most long-term accounts (be they assets or liabilities) run some risk of default. Attentive partners who take the time to examine the balance sheets will inquire into those risks.

Introduction to Schedule K-1

All of the foregoing has dealt with features and preparation of Form 1065: U.S. Partnership Return of Income. As has been

Page 4	SCHEDULE L (FORM 1065)				TAX YEAR
		Beginning of year		End of year	
	Assets	(a)	(b)	(c)	(d)
1	Cash & bank balances	/////		/////	
2	Accounts receivable		/////		/////
	LESS uncollectibles				
3	Inventories	/////		/////	
4	Notes & bonds	/////		/////	
5	Other current assets	/////		/////	
6	Real estate loans	/////		/////	
7	Other investments	/////		/////	
8	Depreciable assets		/////		/////
	LESS prior taken				
9	Depletable assets		/////		/////
	LESS prior taken				
10	Land (at cost)	/////		/////	
11	Amortizable assets		/////		/////
	LESS prior taken				
12	Other assets	/////		/////	
13	**TOTAL ASSETS**	/////		/////	
	Liabilities & Partners' Capital				
14	Accounts payable	/////		/////	
15	Notes payable: < 1 yr	/////		/////	
16	Other liabilities: < 1 yr	/////		/////	
17	Nonrecourse loans	/////		/////	
18	Notes payable: > 1 yr	/////		/////	
19	Other liabilities	/////		/////	
20	PARTNERS' CAPITAL	/////		/////	
21	**TOTAL Liabilities**	/////		/////	

Fig. 9.6 - Edited Contents of Partnership Balance Sheets

stated, the partnership itself is not taxed as an entity. The information on Form 1065 is passed through to the partners where it is taxed at each partner's own individual rates. The consequence is that Form 1065 is an *information* return: not a tax return.

"How is the information passed through to each partner?" you may ask.

Answer: via Schedule K-1 (Form 1065).

Schedule K-1 is titled: **Partner's Share of Income, Credits, Deductions, Etc.** The K-1 is a separate intermediate form of its own. It is "intermediate" between Form 1065 and Form 1040 for each partner. It is a summary of the distributive share of tax information derived from Form 1065 which is intended for Form 1040. It is accompanied by approximately 9,000 words of official instructions.

Among other things, the instructions state that—

*The purpose of Schedule K-1 is to report to you your share of the partnership's income, credits, deductions, etc. **Please keep it for your records. Do not file with your tax return.** A copy has been filed with the IRS. . . . You are liable for your share of the partnership's income, whether or not distributed, and you must include your share on your tax return.*

Schedule K-1 is a very comprehensive tax document. It is prepared by the tax matters partner upon closing the books for each accounting year of the partnership. It is entirely too complex for us to discuss it here in full. Instead, we present only an abbreviated version of its format and contents. This we do in Figure 9.7. Note that Figure 9.7 consists of approximately 50 entry items, and approximately 15 other associated tax forms. It actually covers two full pages (front and back), but we have shown it all in one.

Now you know why we urged earlier that the partnership adopt an accounting year that ends on September 30. The tax matters partner — and his bookkeeper/accountant — need adequate time to compile all the data and make the proper distributive share calculations. This allows 90 days before each partner has to close his own tax books on December 31.

There is a separate Schedule K-1 for each partner. Each K-1 displays each partner's name, address, and (of course) social security number. Approximately midway down on the front page,

Sch. K-1 Form 1065	PARTNER'S DISTRIBUTIVE SHARE ITEMS	Tax Year

Partner's Soc. Sec. No.	Partnership's Fed. I.D. No.
Name & address of partner	Name & address of partnership
Questions, liabilities, & checkboxes ☐ ☐	Questions, percentages, & checkboxes ☐ ☐

Partner's Capital Account							

Pass-through Item	Amount	Forms
Income (Loss) 8 items		Sch. B (1040) Sch. D (1040) Sch. E (1040) Form 4797
Deductions 4 items		Form 8283 Sch. A (1040)
Credits 6 items		Form 3468 Form 5884 Form 8586
Self - Employment 3 items		Sch. SE (1040)
Tax Preferences 6 items		Form 6251
Investment Interest 3 items		Form 4952
Foreign Taxes 5 items		Form 1116
Investment Credit Recapture 5 items		Form 4255
Other Items & Elections as provided by partnership		Form 4136 Form 8271 Form 8275 Form 8308

Fig. 9.7 - Abbreviated Contents of Schedule K-1 (Form 1065)

there is a subschedule: *Analysis of Partner's Capital Account*. This is a summary of each partner's capital participation in the business. You should review carefully your capital account entries, as well as all other entries on the K-1.

If you feel that an error has been made on your K-1, you should contact the tax matters partner. Often, what is believed to be an error is a misunderstanding of how partnership accounting works. It is different — and more complex — than your own individual tax accounting. This is because of the distributive share computations, the pass-through features, and the balance sheet requirements. If you have a negative end-of-year capital account, you pay tax on money you may never see. It was consumed *in* the partnership.

Many Key Questions Asked

Approximately one-third of page 1 of Schedule K-1 is devoted to questions, statements, checkboxes, dollar amounts of liability, and percentage entry lines. There are some 12 to 15 of these informational-type items. We only symbolized these matters in Figure 9.7. It is appropriate, now, to comment on some of the more important of these items.

The very first informational item on the Schedule K-1 is:

This partner is a ☐ *general partner* ☐ *limited partner*
☐ *limited liability company member*

A general partner is one who has equal voice (with other general partners) in the management and control of the business. He is also co-liable for all debts of the partnership. A general partner is not limited in his financial exposure as in the case of a limited partner or an LLC member. Our focus in this book is on general partnerships: partners who conduct an active trade or business domestically and who are not engaged in tax shelters.

When checking the general partner checkbox, three statements follow. These are:

Partner's share of liabilities:
    Nonrecourse $_____
    Qualified nonrecourse $_____
    Other financing $_____

A general partner has to share directly in all of the liabilities of the partnership. Most general partnerships are chronically short of money and have to borrow extensively. There are two types of borrowed money in a partnership, namely: (a) nonrecourse loans and (b) recourse loans. A nonrecourse loan is one which is secured by designated assets and productivity of the partnership. There is no recourse against the personal (nonpartnership) assets of the partners. All partners must share in the nonrecourse liabilities in direct proportion to their ownership of capital. This is why the item "nonrecourse loans" appears on the balance sheets. See line 17 in Figure 9.6.

Each partner's percentage of ownership of capital has to be entered conspicuously in the questions portion of Schedule K-1. This is a rather simple computation to make. If partner B, for example, has a capital account of $10,000, when the total of all partners' capital is $38,000, B's percentage of capital is 26.31% (10,000 ÷ 38,000).

There are two other percentages that have to be identified. These are: (a) % profit sharing, and (b) % loss sharing. If so stated clearly in the partnership agreement, either of these percentages may be any combination that total 100%. There is only one exception. The % of loss sharing cannot produce a pass-through loss that exceeds the amount of a partner's capital that is at risk.

Consider, for example, partner B above with his $10,000 of "at risk" capital. Suppose the partnership agreement allows 80% loss sharing to B. If the business had a net loss for the year of $15,000, B's share of that loss would be $12,000 (80% x $15,000). Since this amount exceeds his risk capital, his share of the partnership loss that passes through to his own tax return (Form 1040) is limited to $10,000. Even for this amount, B has to complete Form 6198 (At-Risk Limitations) and attach it to his Form 1040.

Figuring Each "Distributive Share"

The determination of each partner's tax liability is set forth in Sections 701 through 709 of the tax code. Of particular interest to us at this point is Section 702: *Income and Credits of Partner*. The general rule, subsection (a) thereof says—

In determining his income tax, each partner shall take into account separately his distributive share of the partnership's—

(1)   ordinary income or loss,
(2)   income or loss from rental real estate,
(3)   income or loss from other rental activities,
(4)   net gain or loss from capital assets,
(5)   net gain or loss from section 1231 property,
(6)   net gain or loss from involuntary conversions,
(7)   deductible charitable contributions,
(8)   taxes paid or accrued to foreign countries,
(9)   section 179 expense deduction for recovery property,
(10) depreciation adjustment for property after 1986,
(11) depletion allowance for mines, wells, natural deposits,
(12) amortization of organization fees and other items,
(13) any income, gain, or loss on unrealized receivables and substantially appreciated inventory,
(14) investment interest expense incurred in portfolio investments and net lease property, and
(15) *other items of income, gain, loss, deduction, or credit to the extent prescribed by regulation.*

There is a reason for our citing this long list. It is to convince you that it is not just the ordinary income or loss on page 1 of Form 1065 (Fig. 9.3) that has to be distributively shared. There are many other "distributive share" items as well. This — among other reasons — is why partnership accounting is more complex than a proprietorship . . . or even a corporation (as you will see in the next chapter).

Ordinary income or loss are the most commonly identified sharing items in the partnership agreement. The term "ordinary" refers to the partnership's core business: not its satellite activities. The satellite activities become "other distributive share" items. The agreement is generally silent on these other distributive items. For those items on which the agreement is silent, the distributive share allocation is based on each partner's *ownership interest* in the partnership (Sec. 704(b)). This allocation "shall be determined . . . by taking into account all facts and circumstances."

The two most common facts and circumstances are: (a) each partner's capital account, and (b) each partner's *participating days* in the partnership year. A partner who has risked his capital for 365 days is deserving of a larger distributive share than a partner who has risked his capital for, say, 100 days.

Let us illustrate the distributive share allocation with specific numbers. Consider the following facts and circumstances:

	Capital at risk	Participating days
Partner A	$10,000	250
Partner B	10,000	365
Partner C	18,000	100

The distributive share percentage of any allocable item based on each partner's participating interest is as follows:

Partner A: $10,000 x 250/365(0.6849) = $ 6,849 = 31.45%

Partner B: 10,000 x 365/365(1.0000) = 10,000 = 45.92%

Partner C: 18,000 x 100/365(0.2739) = 4,930 = 22.63%

$38,000 $21,779   100.00%

Whereas the total capital account for all partners is $38,000 the at-risk participating amount is $21,779. Of this amount, partner B's participating interest — for distributive share purposes — is 10,000 ÷ 21,779 or 45.92%. His ownership of capital, however, is 10,000 ÷ 38,000 or 26.31%.

Each distributive share item which is not otherwise identified in the partnership agreement, is allocated according to each partner's participating interest. This is the information which goes on each partner's Schedule K-1 (as per Fig. 9.7). The forms column on the K-1 directs each partner to those tax forms which he must prepare and attach to his own individual Form 1040.

10

FORM 1120 CORPORATIONS

A Corporation Is A Separate Taxable Entity Of Its Own. The Amount Of Tax Is Computed On Form 1120, Filed Each Fiscal Year. This Form Consists Of 4 Pages, 10 Subschedules, And Numerous Other Attachments (Such As, Loss Carrybacks And Carryforwards). Owner-Officers Must Pay Themselves A Salary And Report Same (Plus Their Fringe Benefits) On Form W-2. For Taxable Incomes Over $100,000, Corporate Tax Rates "Jump All Over The Place." However, As Many As 15 Applicable Credits Are Available. Closely-Held Corporations Are Subject To A Flat 35% "Personal Holding Company" Tax.

In this chapter, we focus on small business corporations. If small enough (with 10 or fewer shareholders), such enterprises are referred to as "closely-held" corporations. They are closely-held in the sense that they do not have widely-held public ownership whose shares are traded actively on the various stock exchanges. For our purposes, we are addressing small, privately-held corporations starting up with, say, five owner-shareholders. Very few private businesses start in large corporate form.

Conducting a business in corporate form brings into play more detailed tax accounting than required for proprietorships or partnerships. Note that we say "more detailed": **not** more complex. We think partnership tax accounting is much more complex than corporate accounting. But there are more accounting details (as you'll soon see) for corporations. Consequently, we are going to cover briefly the four-page Form 1120: **U. S. Corporation Income Tax Return.**

Right off, you should note that the word "tax" appears in the official title to Form 1120. This means that a corporation is a taxable entity of its own. A corporation pays a graduated income tax — and other taxes — just like an individual does. This is quite unlike a partnership.

In one sense, there is some tax simplicity in the corporate form. Everything is handled by the corporation. It has its own separate books of account (no pass-throughs involved); it has its own separate tax year (which is on a fiscal basis of its choosing); and it is a "taxpayer" strictly independent of its owners and their taxpaying interests. If properly managed, a corporation can facilitate business growth more flexibly than proprietorships or partnerships.

Immediate Tax Suspicion

A closely-held corporation is immediately tax suspect. The suspicion is particularly intense where the owners are unable — or incapable — of distancing themselves from the corporate entity. While in one sense it is "their" corporation, in another sense it is *not* "their" corporation. It is governmentally watched as an independent taxpayer.

Many small corporations are created in the belief that its owners can perform tax magic behind the corporate shield. They use the corporation as a game of self-dealing in which many personal, nonbusiness expenses are written off against the corporate income. If the corporation makes money, they buy luxury cars and recreational facilities in the corporate name, but only the owners and their family members can use them. If the corporation builds up accumulated earnings, the owners start borrowing from the corporation. They borrow at below-market interest rates or at no interest at all. The loans are seldom paid back to the corporation; they are rolled over year after year. All the while, the owners pay no income tax on the perpetual borrowings from their own corporation.

A corporation has the right to arrange its business affairs in any (otherwise legitimate) manner that will save taxes. But the owners thereof cannot set up a corporation merely for the purpose of saving taxes. The corporation itself must be "real." That is, it must have a genuine business purpose and there must be a sound economic reason for its existence. A closely-held corporation can be disregarded by the IRS if it appears to be used solely as a means of tax avoidance. The Supreme Court so ruled in favor of the IRS to this effect, back in 1940.

In *Higgins v. Smith* , 308 US 473, the Court said—

The Government may look at actualities, and upon determining that the form employed for doing business or carrying out the challenged tax event is unreal or a sham, may sustain or disregard the effect of the fiction as best serves the purposes of the tax statute.

To prevent abuse of the corporate form of business, a number of rather stringent tax rules have been enacted. The gamut runs from Section 531 through 537, and from Section 541 through 547. Illustrative of the point that we are making is Section 533: *Evidence of Purpose to Avoid Income Tax.* In pertinent part, this section reads—

(a) The fact that the earnings and profits of a corporation are permitted to accumulate beyond the reasonable needs of the business shall be determinative of the purpose to avoid the income tax with respect to shareholders.
(b) The fact that any corporation is a mere holding or investment company shall be prima facie evidence of the purpose to avoid the income tax with respect to shareholders.

The significance of the above is that there is just no point in forming a corporation for tax-only reasons. You and your associates must be driven into the corporate route by a true business necessity. Such a necessity could be for competitive reasons, protection against product and worker liabilities, and expansion plans. The most successful small corporations are those which have evolved from prior businesses operating as proprietorships or partnerships.

A Creation Under State Law

A corporation is a legal entity formed, created, and "born" under state law. There is no federal corporation law, as such. This is because every state has its own body of statutes specifically directed at those corporate entities within their state boundaries. Jurisdiction vests in that state where the head office is located, or where the principal place of business is conducted. Every state has its own code of "General Corporation Law."

To form a corporation, written Articles of Incorporation — or other incorporating document — must be filed with the Secretary of State having jurisdiction over the business. This involves a filing fee, a prepaid "franchise tax," and other administrative forms. Instructions and forms can be obtained from the Secretary of State's office in the capital of your state.

Forming a corporation is actually quite simple. Most states require only minimal information in the Articles, such as: (1) name of business, (2) place of business, (3) name of directors, (4) name of "legal representative" and address, (5) nature and purpose of business, (6) amount of initial capitalization, (7) number of initial shares, (8) shareholder voting rights, (9) some reference to the adoption of bylaws, and (10) periodic shareholder meetings. For a small corporation, the Articles could be prepared by any one of the owners without aid of an attorney. Sample forms can be obtained from the Secretary of State or by browsing through the Corporation Code for your state (in any law or reference library).

The nature and purpose of the business can be stated in very broad terms. For example, a perfectly valid statement could be—

The nature of the business, and the objects and purposes proposed to be transacted, promoted and carried on, are to engage in any lawful act or activity for which corporations may be organized under the General Corporation Law of the State of

_____.

In most situations, this statement will pass the filing requirements test. Preparing a 25-page legal dissertation is unnecessary.

There is only one other serious matter that is screened when filing for incorporation. There must be an acknowledgement of the restricted nature of the corporate stock to be issued. Many states have their own corporate securities laws in addition to recognizing federal securities laws. Typically, if stock is held by 25 or fewer persons, it is classed as *restricted stock.* It cannot be sold to, nor offered to the public at large. Restricted stock must be offered back to the corporation, then to other shareholders thereof, before being sold only to close personal associates.

When the Articles of Incorporation are officially accepted, a *Certificate of Incorporation* is issued. A large gold seal is impressed thereon, plus the signature of the Secretary of State. After the legal date of certification, you can commence business and advertise yourself as a "corporation."

Fiscal Year: Indefinite Life

Becoming a corporation is easy. It is when you start operating as a corporation that you enter a new tax world.

The new world starts on the first day of the month in which you are certified as a corporation. If your certification takes place on January 29, for example, your corporate year starts on January 1. This is no different from a calendar year period for individuals.

If, instead, your certification takes place on June 29, your corporation year begins on June 1 and ends on May 30 the following year. You are now on a fiscal year accounting period. The term "fiscal year" means a period of 12 consecutive months ending on the last day of any month other than December. Most corporations operate on a fiscal year basis.

A regular corporation (C-type) is not inhibited from adopting any fiscal year that serves its business interests. If the automatic fiscal year (commencing on date of incorporation) is not to your liking, you can elect another 12-month cycle. But you must do this very early in your startup year. To authenticate your election, you have to call a special meeting of your corporate directors and adopt a resolution setting forth the ending month of your first full fiscal year. Because of employer and other quarterly tax returns, many corporations adopt a fiscal year ending on a calendar quarter (March 31, June 30, or September 30).

When an automatic fiscal year is altered to coincide with the ending month of a calendar quarter, a *short period* corporate tax return (Form 1120) has to be filed. If the short period is less than 45 days, a new corporation can "suspend its books" — so to speak — and file a blank Form 1120. You write across its face (in bold red letters): NO INCOME. NEW BUSINESS JUST STARTED. This action is permitted by Code Section 443: short period returns for taxpayers not in existence for entire (first) taxable year.

Once your fiscal year cycle is straightened out, as a corporation, your business has indefinite life. This means that as long as you pay the annual registration fee (to the Secretary of State of the state of incorporation), your corporate charter remains valid indefinitely. There is no preassigned or predetermined expiration date. Real corporations are formed with the intention of continuing in business into the far distant future.

Introduction to Form 1120

As stated earlier, Form 1120 (U. S. Corporation Income Tax Return) consists of four full pages of tax information. The four pages are partitioned into 12 subschedules totaling nearly 200 entry lines. There are over 20,000 words of official instructions for preparing Form 1120. Obviously, we cannot do justice to this form in this chapter.

Our focus is not on how to prepare Form 1120, but merely to acquaint you with it. We want to introduce some of its peculiarities. We also want to point out some of the differences between this form and those used by proprietorships and partnerships. This way, you may better appreciate the comprehensiveness of Form 1120 and why corporations require so much accounting detail.

Many small corporation owners take a look at Form 1120 and literally throw up their hands. Their first reaction is: "That's not for me; that's what tax accountants are for!"

Yes, . . . perhaps.

But as an officer of the corporation, you are going to have to sign Form 1120 . . . *under penalties of perjury*. We think you should know at least something of what you are signing.

Accordingly, we present in Figure 10.1 an outline of all the subschedules on Form 1120. We show the heading block and signature block as though all subschedules were on page 1. This, of course, is not the case. They are on four pages. Please take a moment to read through the titles of the subschedules. Then look at the very top of Figure 10.1.

We confront, now, the first peculiarity of Form 1120. There is a preprinted calendar year in bold black figures in the top right corner of page 1 (as is the case with all tax forms). For illustration purposes, we show the year 1998. Then, immediately below the head title, there is space for entering the fiscal year: *beginning* _____, *ending* _____. This creates a lot confusion as to which tax year is involved.

Ordinarily, one thinks of the ending year as the year for which a tax return is prepared. In the case of Form 1120, however, the preprinted calendar year signifies the **beginning** of the fiscal year. Let us illustrate.

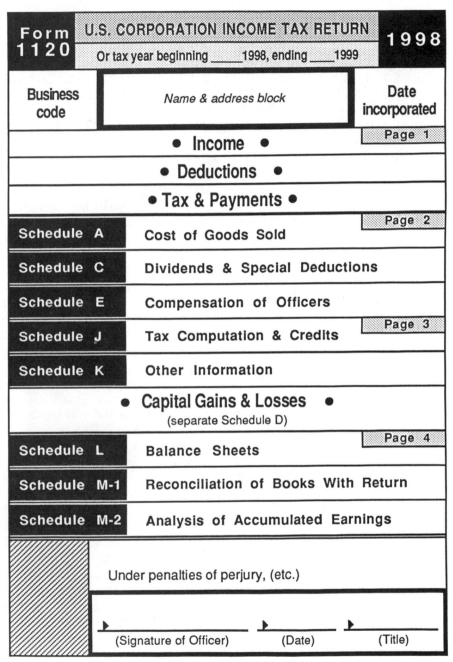

Form 1120	U.S. CORPORATION INCOME TAX RETURN	1998
	Or tax year beginning _____ 1998, ending _____ 1999	

Business code	Name & address block	Date incorporated

• Income •   Page 1

• Deductions •

• Tax & Payments •
                                                  Page 2

Schedule A	Cost of Goods Sold
Schedule C	Dividends & Special Deductions
Schedule E	Compensation of Officers
	Page 3
Schedule J	Tax Computation & Credits
Schedule K	Other Information

• Capital Gains & Losses •
(separate Schedule D)
                                                  Page 4

Schedule L	Balance Sheets
Schedule M-1	Reconciliation of Books With Return
Schedule M-2	Analysis of Accumulated Earnings

Under penalties of perjury, (etc.)

▶ _____ ▶ _____ ▶ _____
(Signature of Officer)   (Date)   (Title)

Fig. 10.1 - Summary Contents of a C-Corporation Tax Return

Suppose your fiscal year begins July 1, 1998 and
1999. Which preprinted calendar year tax form do yc
or 1999?

Answer: 1998 — the year in which your fiscal year

As an individual, your 1998 Form 1040 covers the
period ending December 1998. Your 1999 Form 1040
period ending December 1999. Yet, as a corporation, for t
ending June 1999, you file a tax form preprinted with 199
this make sense?

We are calling your attention to this anomaly because it is
trivial matter. Today, the IRS is terribly automated
computerized. If you try using ending year common sense, an
the wrong preprinted-year tax forms, you will be comp
terrorized. There will be endless IRS computer mismatch
problems. So, do take heed. Use the computer consiste
preprinted-year tax forms.

Administratively, there is a reason for this filing-year anomaly
for corporations. In our example above, the 1999 tax forms are not
government printed until very late in 1998 or early in 1999. For
fiscal years ending in March, June, or September of 1999, no 1999
tax forms would be available. Hence, the 1998 already printed
forms have to be used.

Income & Deduction Differences

The profit and loss aspects of a corporation are more comparable
to those of a partnership than to a proprietorship. This is because
the income and deductions subschedules are strikingly similar.
There are significant differences, of course.

Both partnerships and corporations have multiple sources of
income against which prioritized deductions are allowed. The key
difference is the net income (or loss) after deductions. For
corporations, the net income (profit) is *taxable income*. The amount
of tax is computed elsewhere on Form 1120, and then is entered
immediately below the taxable income line as total tax.

If there is a net loss on Form 1120, it is not taxable. It rides on
the books as a *net operating loss* (NOL). For new startup
corporations, the NOL can be carried forward as another deduction
for the following year. It does not pass through to the owners in
any way.

Before touching on a few other differences, we should present
Figure 10.2. It is a slightly edited version of the income and

Form 1120	CORPORATION INCOME TAX RETURN	Tax Year
Income		Amount
1	Gross receipts (less returns & allowances)	
2	Cost of goods sold	
3	Gross profit (subtract line 2 from line 1)	
4	Gross dividends (Schedule C)	
5	Gross interest	
6	Gross rents	
7	Gross royalties	
8	Net capital gain (Schedule D)	
9	Other net gain or loss (Form 4797)	
10	Other income (attach statement)	
11	///////// TOTAL INCOME ➤	
Deductions		Amount
12	Compensation of officers (Schedule E)	
13	Salaries & wages (other than officers)	
14	Repairs	
15	Bad debts (specific write-offs)	
16	Rents	
17	Taxes (other than income taxes)	
18	Interest	
19	Contributions (max. 10% of taxable income)	
20	Depreciation (Form 4562)	
21	Amortization (Form 4562)	
22	Depletion	
23	Advertising	
24	Pension & profit sharing plans	
25	Employee benefit programs	
26	Other deductions (attach statement)	
27	///////// TOTAL DEDUCTIONS ➤	
28	**Taxable Income - Tentative** ▶ ▶ ▶	
29	**LESS Special Deductions**	/////////
	a. Net operating Loss (attach statement)	
	b. Dividends deduction (Schedule C)	
30	**TAXABLE INCOME - Net** ▶ ▶ ▶ ▶ ▶	

Fig. 10.2 - Sequence to Taxable Income on Form 1120

deduction lines on Form 1120. For comparison, you might want to glance back momentarily at Figures 9.4 and 9.5 (for partnerships).

One of the first differences you may note in Figure 10.2 is the *dividends* income line. It is accompanied by the parenthetical instruction: "Schedule C." Do not confuse this Schedule C with the Schedule C (Form 1040) of a proprietorship. Schedule C (Form 1120) serves a totally different purpose (as discussed below).

Another income difference to note on Form 1120 is *net capital gain*. This is the gain derived from the sale of capital assets of the corporation (not goods or services). Interestingly, there is no income line provision for net capital loss. What happens if there is a net capital loss for the year?

The net capital loss of a corporation is carried back three years to combine with any capital gain for those years. If there is no prior capital gain, the net capital loss is carried forward for five years to combine with any likely capital gain for those years.

Are you beginning to sense the different machinations of corporate tax accounting?

On the deductions side of the ledger, the principal difference between partnerships and corporations is the treatment of owner salaries. If a shareholder in a corporation is also an officer of that corporation, he/she must be paid a salary. The salaries of all owner-officers are displayed on a separate subschedule (Schedule E) on Form 1120. Each officer's name, social security number, percentage of time devoted to business, percentage of stock ownership, and amount of compensation are shown. All compensation to officers is deductible against the income of the corporation.

On Form 1120, when the total deductions are subtracted from total income, the taxable income at that point is a *tentative* amount. We so indicated this at line 28 in Figure 10.2. Against this tentative taxable income, there are two entirely new deductions. These are—

(a) The NOL deduction (carryover or carryback)

(b) Special deductions (Schedule C)

When these two deductions are subtracted from the tentative taxable income, the net becomes the taxable income.

Generally, a corporation may carry an NOL back to each of three years preceding the year of the loss, and carry it over to each of 15 years following the year of the loss (Sec. 172(b)). There are deviations from this general rule for product liability losses, foreign expropriation losses, and nuclear decommissioning losses. When claiming an NOL deduction, a comprehensive carryback-carryover statement of computations must be attached to Form 1120.

Schedule C (1120): Uniquely Special

On two occasions above, there was mention of "Schedule C" (Form 1120). In Figure 10.1 we identified this subschedule as *Dividends and Special Deductions*. And, indeed, it is. This is a class of deductions which applies only to corporations: not to partnerships; not to proprietorships.

These special dividend deductions are prescribed by Sections 243 through 247 of the tax code. They are pronounced "shall be allowed" by Section 241. This section reads in part as—

In addition to the deductions provided [elsewhere], *there shall be allowed as deductions in computing taxable income the items specified in this part.*

The tax code phrase "this part" refers to the following sections (among others):

Sec. 243 — Dividends Received from Other Corporations
Sec. 244 — Dividends Received from Public Utilities
Sec. 245 — Dividends Received from Foreign Corporations
Sec. 246 — Dividends from Debt Financed Stock
Sec. 247 — Dividends from Preferred Stock of Public Utilities

All of this dividend income to a corporation is subject to a deduction varying from 40% to 100%. The 100% deduction applies to affiliated corporations and wholly-owned subsidiaries. Otherwise, the deduction is scaled from 40% to 80% depending on the extent of ownership in other corporate entities.

This special dividend deduction tempts many small corporations to invest heavily into large domestic, foreign, and public utility corporations. In some cases, this temptation is the sole motivating factor for incorporating versus not incorporating.

Caution. There is a tax trap for you. Ask yourself: "What happens to the 40% to 100% untaxed dividend income that is corporatively received?"

Answer: The untaxed dividends are passed through to the owner-officers as salaries, or declared as dividends to all shareholders. In either case, they are subject to ordinary income tax by the individual recipients. Surely you did not think that 40% to 100% of your corporate income as dividends received would never be taxed, did you?

In reality, small businesses just starting up are unable to take advantage of the special deductions in Schedule C (1120). Most startup businesses tend to be undercapitalized. Rarely is there excess capital available to invest in other corporations which pay dividends.

Balance Sheet Comprehensiveness

All filers of Form 1120 must complete Schedule L: *Balance Sheets*. This schedule constitutes a complete financial statement of the corporate entity for each fiscal year. It is very comprehensive.

Because of its basic importance to corporate tax accounting, we present in Figure 10.3 an exact replica of the line items on Schedule L (on page 4 of Form 1120). For space reasons, we have abridged the entry columns. Otherwise, the line items and the sequence numbering are exact. We are doing this because we want to point out a few items which are novel to corporations.

Small, closely-held corporations tend to engage — indiscriminately — in personal loans back and forth between the corporation and its stockholders. The loans tend to be at below market rates of interest or at no interest at all. Also, the loans tend not to be properly documented. Often, the loans are just penciled book entries which are erased on the verbal say of the principal owners.

To prevent excessive looseness in stockholder loans accounting, Schedule L (1120) requires recordation of these loans at items 6 (TO stockholders) and 18 (FROM stockholders) . . . in Figure 10.3.

In addition, there is Section 7872 (Treatment of Loans With Below-Market Interest Rates) to contend with. Enacted in 1984, this tax law says, in effect, that *applicable federal rates* of interest must be used. If not timely used, the IRS can apply these rates retroactively to all stockholder loans made after June 6, 1984. There is, however, a $10,000 de minimis exception for compensation-related and corporate-shareholder loans.

At item 22 (in Fig. 10.3) the entry reads: Paid-in or capital surplus. This, in effect, is the current book value of corporate stock in excess of its value at time of issue (item 21). This "surplus" is the unrealized portion of capital gain not identified elsewhere on Schedule L. This surplus derives from the appreciation in corporate

Schedule L	BALANCE SHEETS		Form 1120 Page 4
		Beginning of year	End of year
	Assets		
1	Cash on hand		
2	Trade notes and accounts receivable		
	a. Less allowance for bad debts		
3	Inventories		
4	Federal and state government obligations		
5	Other current assets (attach schedule)		
6	Loans TO stockholders		
7	Mortgage and real estate loans		
8	Other investments (attach schedule)		
9	Buildings and other depreciable assets		
	a. Less accumulated depreciation		
10	Depletable assets		
	a. Less accumulated depletion		
11	Land (net of any amortization)		
12	Intangible assets (amortizable only)		
	a. Less accumulated amortization		
13	Other assets (attach schedule)		
14	TOTAL ASSETS ━━━━━▶		
	Liabilities		
15	Accounts payable		
16	Notes payable in less than 1 year		
17	Other current liabilities (attach schedule)		
18	Loans FROM stockholders		
19	Notes payable in 1 year or more		
20	Other liabilities (attach schedule)		
21	Capital stock: a. Preferred Stock		
	b. Common Stock		
22	Paid-in or capital surplus		
23	Retained earnings - appropriated		
24	Retained earnings - unappropriated		
25	Less cost of treasury stock		
26	TOTAL LIABILITIES ━━━━━▶		

> > > > > > > > > > > > > > > > > and stock holders equity

Fig. 10.3 - Items Listed on Form 1120 Balance Sheets

property values and the increasing net worth of the business. This is a "balancing entry" which changes from year to year. In contrast, item 21 remains fixed.

At items 23 and 24 , the entries read respectively: Retained earnings — Appropriated/Unappropriated. Retained earnings are those profits in a corporation which have not been distributed to shareholders as dividends. "Appropriated" retained earnings are those which are earmarked for specific spending plans of the business, such as, for new equipment, new buildings, new markets.

"Unappropriated" retained earnings are excess money floating around in the corporation with no earmarked business purpose in mind. This money is called *accumulated earnings*. This money comes under the watchful eye of the IRS.

If your accumulated earnings exceed $150,000 (for pure-service corporations) or $250,000 (for manufacturing and retail corporations), a penalty tax applies. The penalty for accumulating excess earnings in a corporation is 40% (Sec. 531). The purpose of this penalty is to arm-twist corporate directors into distributing these earnings to individual shareholders where it can be income taxed.

Three Separate Taxes Apply

There are actually three income taxes that apply to corporations. These are

1. Regular tax   —   Schedule J (Form 1120)
2. Minimum tax   —   Form 4626 (to be attached)
3. PHC tax   —   Schedule PH (Form 1120)

Unless there is zero or negative taxable income, at least one of these taxes applies. In some (rare) cases, all three may apply *simultaneously*! So, if you are going to incorporate for tax-saving reasons, you had better think again.

The regular corporate tax is based on a graduated rate schedule. The lowest rate is 15% on taxable incomes up to $50,000. For taxable incomes over $100,000, the rate can go to 35% . . . plus an "additional tax" of 5%. When the tax is computed, it is entered on Schedule J of Form 1120.

The corporate minimum tax is an "alternate" tax designed to defeat the extensive use of "tax preferences." Tax preference deductions include accelerated depreciation, certain amortization and depletion, installment sales, research expenditures, environmental matters, bad debt loss reserves, and "excess book income." The tax is 25% of the preference deductions which exceed $40,000 and 20% if they exceed $150,000.. The minimum tax is computed by using Form 4626 (Minimum Tax—Corporations) and attaching it to Form 1120. At the same time, an entry is made on Schedule J (1120).

The letters "PHC" above stand for: Personal Holding Company. A personal holding company is any corporation which takes on an increasingly passive role in its type of income sources. The PHC tax applies to those corporations whose total income consists of 60% or more from the following sources:

(a) Dividends and interest
(b) Rents from real estate
(c) Rents from movie film
(d) Mineral, oil, & gas royalties
(e) Copyright royalties
(f) Personal service contracts

. . . and other sources prescribed by Section 543 (PHC income). Closely-held corporations often "slip into" the PHC mode without being aware that the owners will be surtaxed.

The PHC tax is designed specifically for closely-held corporations. These are corporations where five or fewer individuals own more than 50% of its stock. The PHC tax rate is a flat 35% on all "undistributed" personal holding company income. The tax is computed by preparing a separate Schedule PH, then entering the amount on Schedule J of Form 1120.

Applicable Credits

There is one area in which corporations have a slight tax edge over partnerships and proprietorships. This is in the area of tax credits. A "credit" is a dollar-for-dollar offset (subtraction) against the computed tax. It is not that the credits are designed to favor corporations (the credits are available to all forms of business), it is just that corporations engage in a greater diversity of activities where the credits are applicable.

Altogether, there are about 15 forms of tax credits which can be used to reduce the *regular* (normal) income tax. The number changes slightly from time to time, and some produce no significant tax impact, The eight most useful of these credits are:

(1) Foreign tax credit—for payment of income tax to a foreign country [Sec. 27; Form 1118]

(2) General business credit—for various unused, repealed, and specialized credits [Sec. 38; Form 3800]

(3) Alcohol fuel credit—for using alcohol as a fuel mixture in highway vehicles [Sec. 40; Form 6478]

(4) Qualified research credit—for increasing in-house research into new products [Sec. 41; Form 6765]

(5) Low-income housing credit—for construction and improvement of low cost housing [Sec. 42; Form 8586]

(6) Targeted jobs credit—for hiring and training disadvantaged persons [Sec. 51; Form 5884]

(7) Prior-year minimum tax credit—for "double taxation" on preference income [Sec. 53; Form 8827]

(8) Possessions tax credit—for taxable income derived in U.S. possessions [Sec. 936; Form 5735]

Be sure to notice above that every tax credit requires the preparation of a designated tax form of its own. Tax credits are never automatic. If you are eligible for any of them, you must stake your claim with the proper form.

Also be aware that all credits listed above offset (subtract from) the normal/regular tax only. The **do not** reduce the alternate minimum tax (AMT) nor the personal holding company (PHC) tax. The sequence of application of the credits is—

Step 1 — Determine regular tax
Step 2 — List and add all credits
Step 3 — *Subtract* Step 2 from Step 1
Step 4 — Determine AMT tax
Step 5 — Determine PHC tax
Step 6 — Total tax: ADD Steps 3, 4, & 5

The effect of Step 4 (alternate minimum tax) is that it often "wastes" some, most, or all of the otherwise allowable credits. In other words, when AMT applies, it can defeat the credits. When this happens, the wasted/unused credits can be carried back three years and carried forward 15 years to offset other-year taxes. The provisions for doing so are set forth in Section 39 of the tax code (*carryback and carryforward of unused credits*).

11

COMPENSATION OF OWNERS

Because Of Ownership Control And Self-Interest, An Owner's Compensatory Forms Are More Closely Tax Scrutinized Than Nonowner Employees. Business Meals, Entertainment, And Vacations Are Virtually "No-No." When Employing One's Spouse And Children, Their Training And Capabilities Must Be Matched To Actual Services Performed. Under Stringent Qualifying Rules, Most Owner Benefits Must Be NONDISCRIMINATORY With Respect To Employees. By A Combination Of Pension, Profit-Sharing, And Deferred Compensation Plans, As Much As $30,000 Can Be "Trusteed" Away Each Year For An Owner's Own Old Age And Retirement.

As reward for their efforts, the owners of a business want to know two things. One: "How much money can I pull out of the business for myself?" Two: "How can I pay the minimum tax on the money I draw?"

The answer to the first question depends on the form of business and the degree of its success. The answer to the second question depends on your taking advantage of: (a) "safe" fringe benefits, (b) family dilution techniques, and (c) pension and profit-sharing plans.

We have purposely framed these two questions and answers. We have done this so as to focus this chapter on the relationship between the owner (or owners) and his/her (or their) business. After all, the purpose in starting one's business (in addition to a livelihood) is to make money and keep as much of that money as possible for one's self. Human self-interest is central to the motivation for starting any business.

Very few persons — no matter how upright they may be as citizens — go into business simply to generate tax revenue for government. Such revenue is strictly a by-product. The underlying purpose of any business is to generate money for the enjoyment of life, and to prepare for one's old age and retirement. All of this is what we mean by "compensation of owners."

Owners Are "Naturally Suspect"

Owners of a business, regardless of its form, are natural targets for tax suspicion. This is because owners control the business: its income, its assets, and its expenditures. The owners are the ones taking the risk. Because so, they have the greatest self-interest at stake. The IRS knows this.

Consequently, in the processing of tax returns, an owner's return is screened more closely than a nonowner's return. The screening focuses primarily on the adequacy of personal income reported, and on the extent of personal benefit expenditures claimed. There is a perpetual undercurrent of bureaucracy suspicion that an owner is "trying to get away with something."

All tax returns are "profiled" and classified before they go through the IRS screening process. This way, the screeners — both human and electronic — concentrate on selected items and "measure" them against quantitative standards. These are probability tests developed over years of screening profiled returns for additional revenue.

If a business owner's return is selected for examination, there is an additional personal questionnaire involved. This is Form 4822: *Statement of Annual Estimated Personal and Family Expenses.* Some 35 preprinted entry lines are involved, plus blank lines for the hand entry of other items that a revenue agent may be curious about. The tax presumption behind Form 4822 is that, somehow, you are "skimming the business." You are using the business to pay for personal and family expenses.

Typical of such presumed skimming items are expenditures for—

- Barber, beauty shop, & cosmetics
- Clothing, laundry, & dry cleaning
- Furniture, appliances, & fixtures

• Home repairs & improvements
• Recreation, entertainment, & vacations

How much was paid for by check or credit card, and how much was paid by cash? The presumption is that any amount paid for by cash was skimmed from the business. If you claim that all was paid by check or credit card, and you do not have itemized receipts, the presumption again is that you skimmed the business for these personal items.

If you object too confrontationally to this invasion of your privacy and presumption of innocence, Section 262 of the tax code may be cited to you. This section reads—

Except as otherwise provided, no deduction shall be allowed for personal, living, or family expenses.

Regulation 1.262-1 amplifies on this wording. It gives the impression that the IRS can search your entire home and frisk all members of your family.

You can — and should — refuse to comply with Form 4822. Do this on the grounds that Section 262 is positioned in the tax code under Subchapter B (Taxable Income), Part IX: ITEMS NOT DEDUCTIBLE. Therefore, you can take the stance that if you are not claiming these items on your personal or business tax returns, the IRS is out of order in asking for them. But, do be sure that you definitely are not claiming them as deductible expenses.

Limit "Meals & Entertainment"

Every business owner has a universal desire. He wants to build up the goodwill of the business in the hopes that it will grow and prosper. The ordinary "tools" for this are business meals, small gifts, and social entertainment. Every business does it . . . more or less. But if the owner of a business himself participates in the goodwill expenditures, said expenses are inhumanly scrutinized.

Previously, we touched on the stringency of documentation and the otherwise disallowance of TME expenses (travel, meals, and entertainment). Because these items will be scrutinized mercilessly, we suggest that as an owner you pursue a policy of limited participation in business meals and entertainment. You may allow these for your employees and nonemployees (provided they submit documented expense vouchers to you), but limit them for yourself.

Travel on business (away from home overnight) is another matter. Compared to meals, gifts, and entertainment, business travel is more conveniently documented. Besides, extensive travel by small business owners is not all that frequent.

The principal reason we urge limiting your meals and entertainment (M&E) is Section 274 (*Disallowance of Certain Entertainment, Etc., Expenses*). This tax rule targets gifts, entertainment, amusement, vacation, recreation, cruise ships, food, beverages, sports tickets, and so on. As an owner of a business, if you participate in these affairs, you will be "beaten over the head" with Section 274. Revenue agents are taught to believe that no business is M&E clean.

Section 274 consists of 15 subsections comprising approximately 5,000 words. Its basic thrust is that M&E is a "No-No." This is set forth in subsection 274(d): *Substantiation Required*, which reads in part as—

> *No deduction or credit shall be allowed . . . unless the taxpayer substantiates by adequate records or by sufficient evidence corroborating—*
>> *(A) the amount of such expense or other item,*
>> *(B) the* [date], *time and place* [involved],
>> *(C) the business purpose of the expense or other item,*
>> *(D) the business relationship to the taxpayer of persons entertained, using the facility or property, or receiving the gift.*

Even after documenting all M&E, only 50% is deductible [Sec. 274(n)]! This is so whether you or your business picks up the tab.

In short, as owner of a business, discipline yourself against "wining and dining" at the expense of your business. The opportunities that you've heard of in the past are gone now. You are expected to absorb certain "no-no" benefits because there are other statutory benefits which are "safe."

Nondiscriminatory Insurance Plans

Although M&E expenditures are scrutinized mercilessly, there are a number of other benefits which are quite acceptable . . . and nontaxable. An overview of these safe benefits is presented in Figure 11.1. Foremost are certain insurance plans.

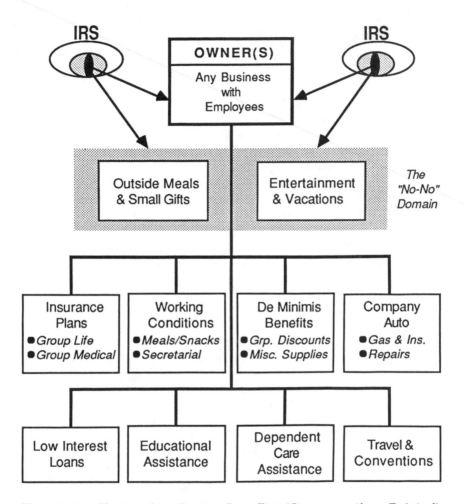

Fig. 11.1 - Nontaxable Owner Benefits (Compensation Related)

Many businesses, large as well as small, offer various insurance plans to their owners and employees. This is done to take advantage of group rates, as well as to assure piece of mind during employment. Some of the plans are statutorily acceptable; some are not. The acceptable ones are those which are characterized as *nondiscriminatory*. Nondiscriminatory plans do not substantially favor owners at the expense of employees.

Company-paid insurance plans are in the form of compensation which, ordinarily, would be includible in the recipient's gross income. However, there are two types of insurance which are statutorily recognized as *exclusions from income*. These two types are:

1. Group-term life insurance   [Sec. 79]
2. Group accident and health   [Sec. 106]

Section 79 (Group-term Life Insurance Purchased for Employees) allows an employer to pay premiums on policies with face values up to $50,000 without requiring those premiums to be reported as income to the employee. For coverage in excess of $50,000, the excess premiums are reported as income on each employee's Form W-2. The "catch" here is that the insured person must be an **employee**. This rules out self-employed owners of proprietorships and some partnerships. Otherwise, the premiums paid are deductible by the business.

Section 106 (Contributions by Employer to Accident and Health Plans) also permits the business to pay the premiums (as deductible expenses) without reporting the premiums as income to the employee. If the plan is nondiscriminatory and provides continuous coverage, the owners (as active participants in the business) may also be covered. On this point, Section 106(a) specifically says—

Gross income of an employee does not include employer-provided coverage under an accident or health plan.

But, again, only employees (including owner-employees) are benefited. All other insurance plans paid for by the business must be related directly and specifically to the business itself. There can be no spillover of benefits whatsoever to the owners, be they owner-employees or self-employeds. This is particularly true for "key person" insurance, disability insurance, hazard insurance, liability insurance, and performance insurance. As an owner, don't let yourself ever succumb to the temptation to include in your business insurance programs coverage for homeowner's insurance, personal auto insurance, and flight insurance for family vacations. Business-necessitated insurance is referred to as "Section 162 plans" (ordinary and necessary business expenses).

"Safe Harbor" Benefits

There are at least five other statutory areas where owners (as active participants) may derive "compensation related" benefits which are tax free. The catch, again, is that the programs must be nondiscriminatory and they should be in writing. If these and other conditions are met, payment for the benefits are deductible expenses to the business. Furthermore, the business cost of the benefits is not includible in the gross income of the recipients (be they owners, officers, employees, or nonemployees). We call these "safe harbor" benefits because they are statutorily sanctioned.

The five particular benefits that we have in mind are—

(1) Sec. 119   —   Meals served on business premises
(2) Sec. 127   —   Up to $5,250 in "educational assistance"
(3) Sec. 129   —   Up to $5,000 for "dependent care"
(4) Sec. 132   —   "Working condition" fringes
(5) Sec. 7872 —   Up to $10,000 interest-free loans

A word or two on each of these statutory benefits is instructive.

Section 119 says, in essence, that if meals are served on business premises for business reasons, and are paid for by the business, they are not taxable benefits to the meal recipients. Many small businesses have designated areas where food (packaged or catered), snacks, and beverages can be consumed. An owner is not disbarred from having business meals on his own premises. If an owner normally stays at his place of business after hours, meals served during those hours also would qualify. This could be opportunity to offset some of the (previously mentioned) owner-absorbed meals and entertainment consumed off-premises.

Section 127 permits a business to pay for tuition, books, supplies, and tools (up to $5,250) for instruction that improves or develops the capabilities of an employee. The only requirement is that instruction be at an educational institution, and that the course(s) not be in sports, games, hobbies, or recreational activities.

Section 129 permits a business to pay up to $5,000 in "assistance" to an employee for the care of a child, incapacitated spouse, or elderly parent . . . while the employee is at work.

Section 132 addresses "working condition" and "de minimus" fringes. These are incidental benefits that are part of the everyday working environment of each particular type of business. The direct cost of these benefits is obscure and is generally part of the ordinary business operation (employee discounts, for example).

Section 7872 (Treatment of Loans with Below-Market Interest Rates) is probably more directed at owners rather than employees. Compensation-related loans up to $10,000 may be interest free. For loans up to $100,000 the interest must equal the"net investment income" from such loans. For loans in excess of $100,000, the interest must be imputed at the "applicable federal rate." These are called *gift loans* because no collateral, security, or qualifying (personal) financial statements are required. The thrust of Section 7872 is that an owner borrowing money from his own business is acceptable, so long as the interest rules are followed and there is written documentation on each loan.

A "Company-Provided" Auto

Every owner of a business needs a car for business purposes. It is virtually impossible to conduct any business today by remaining on business premises all day long, every day, without ever leaving to attend to some business matter. Consequently, a business car is a "working condition" necessity. [Sec. 132(a)(3)]

The question in every owner's mind is: "How can the business provide a car for my use, with the least record-keeping fuss and bother?"

Basically, every company-provided auto is a taxable fringe benefit. The taxable portion is the personal use of the car: not its business use. The taxable portion is satisfied in one of two ways. It is treated either as—

(a) compensation to the owner (by the business), which is reported as income on his personal return, or

(b) reimbursement to the business (by the owner) which is reported as income on the business return.

For overall simplicity in record-keeping, the compensation treatment is preferred. The owner is taxed on a relatively minor amount, whereas the business gets a 100% writeoff for all expenses of operating the vehicle. The business, however, does not get a deduction for the additional compensation reported by the owner.

There are two compensation reporting methods, namely:

(1) "commute only" with a utility type auto, and

(2) "annual lease" of a luxury type auto

There is also a third method (standard mileage rate) but it is more applicable to employees than to owners.

In the "commute only" method, the business buys a utility car (say, a $15,000 vehicle) and assigns it to the owner. A written contract is prepared which prohibits the car from being used for personal purposes other than commuting between home and business. The contract also requires that the owner have a personal vehicle of his own, for family and vacation use. If these conditions are met, the business reports $3 per commute day as additional taxable income to the owner. Typically, this would be $750 per year (for 250 commute days).

In the "annual lease" method, the business buys or leases a luxury car (say, a $35,000 vehicle) and assigns it to the owner. The owner is allowed to use the car for other than commuting. However, he must report to the business each year his true percentage of personal use of the vehicle. Say this personal use is 25%. Based on IRS tables, the annual lease value of a $35,000 auto is $9,250. At 25% personal use, the amount of $2,313 per year ($9,250 x 25%) would be reported by the business as additional income to the owner.

In both methods (commute only and annual lease), the business deducts 100% of all operating expenses on the vehicle. For convenience in this regard, many businesses obtain gas and repair credit cards and assign them to the drivers of each company-provided vehicle. This, in itself, is a significant tax benefit to the business owner(s).

Livelihood Compensation Differences

All of the foregoing (nontaxable) benefits are classed as *nonlivelihood* compensation. Except for the small taxable portions which we have identified, all expenditures therewith are fully deductible by the business. This is true whether the business is a proprietorship, a partnership, or a corporation. The only requirement is that the business have employees other than the owners themselves. A business with owners only would be hard pressed to qualify for these nondiscriminatory employee benefit programs.

When we get into livelihood compensation, the form in which a business is conducted does make a difference. Except in the corporate form, the participating owners are not employees. Their livelihood depends on the net profit or loss of the business. The differences in livelihood compensation for the different forms of business are summarized in Figure 11.2. As self-evident therein, at the "bottom line" all such compensation is fully taxable.

In a sole proprietorship, the owner's livelihood compensation is simply the net earnings from the business. The true amount of his net earnings is not known until the end of the taxable year. What does he do for livelihood purposes during the intervening 12 months?

Answer: He makes an "anticipatory draw" from time to time throughout the year. Even if he does not need to do this for livelihood reasons (assuming he lived off of his savings), he would have to do it for estimated tax *prepayment* purposes. The owner of a proprietorship is not on a regular salary; therefore, he is not subject to periodic withholdings. But he is subject to mandatory prepayments of his tax. He makes these prepayments on quarterly voucher forms 1040-ES. We'll describe these voucher forms in Chapter 12 (Compliance Matters).

In a general partnership, each partner's livelihood compensation is his "distributive share" of the net earnings of the business. Similarly to a proprietorship, the partners are not on a salary. They can, however, receive "guaranteed payments." They can use these payments, if not for livelihood, for their estimated tax prepayments. If the partnership engages bona fide employees, the guaranteed payments to partners could be structured as wages, subject to all withholdings.

In a C corporation, the owners — as officers/employees — draw a "stipulated salary" for their livelihood compensation. They can do this in anticipation of the corporate net profit for the year. Or, as many closely-held corporations do, the owners agree to a nominal salary for the year, and then assign themselves a *bonus* at the end of the year, when the profit picture is better known. The salary and bonus are subject to full withholdings for both income and social security/medicare taxes.

Any year-end bonus must be based on the individual productivity of the owners and *not* on the number of shares that each holds. Any bonus based on ownership share will be tax treated as *dividends*. A dividend is not a deductible expense of the corporation, whereas a bonus is deductible. A bonus is compensation for personal services, whereas a dividend is compensation for capital invested. A dividend is income taxed twice: once at the corporate level and again at the individual shareholder level. A dividend, however, is not subject to social security and medicare tax, whereas a bonus is so taxed.

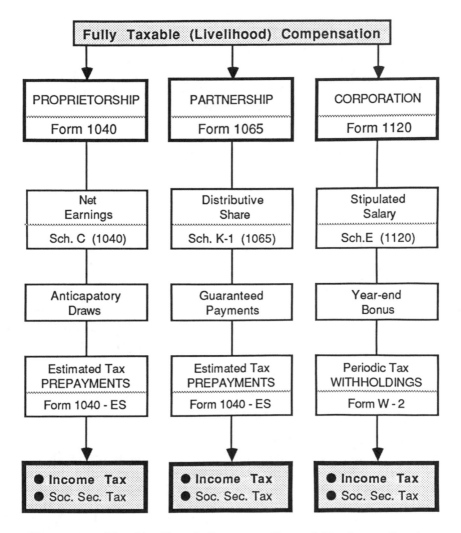

Fig. 11.2 - The Livelihood Compensation of Business Owners

Employing Spouse & Children

In successful businesses the practice is to employ family members — particularly the spouse and children — of the owner(s). This is good practice where there is genuine business need for the training, experience, and capabilities of selected family members.

Actual services must be performed, and the compensation must be reasonable. Here, the term "reasonable" means comparable to that paid to nonfamily employees for the same tasks.

There must be a bona fide employer-employee relationship between each owner and his/her spouse and children. If such relationship exists, there can be some tax *dilution* benefits to the owner. But one has to be certain that the dilution is genuine. It cannot be disguise for personal expenses, family chores, children's education, or gifts to minors.

When employing one's spouse in a business, there is virtually no income tax dilution. Most married persons file joint returns. Consequently, any diminution of the owner's income by the amount paid to his spouse is simply added back into the joint gross income. The key benefit with spousal employees is the social security tax and retirement plan deductions.

Ordinarily, when starting a business, one "employs" his (or her) spouse on a noncompensatory basis. That is, the spouse helps out doing odd jobs, part time. But as the business gets going the spouse may want a separate social security/medicare base of her (or his) own. If so, the spouse can be treated as an "independent contractor" in a proprietorship, an "associate partner" in a partnership, or as a "regular employee" in a corporation. However treated, there is social security/medicare tax on the spousal earnings.

Regardless of the form of business, an employed spouse can become a participant in an employer-sponsored retirement plan. This, in effect, becomes additional deferred compensation which may be tax beneficial to an owner.

When it comes to employing dependent children of the owner(s) of a business, there is real skepticism and challenge by the IRS. Do the children perform useful productive services for the business? Or, are they performing parental-directed chores which they would be expected to do, whether the parent(s) owned the business or not? Is their compensation just enough to offset other child-rearing costs such as education, tutoring, recreation, sports activities? Do the children file tax returns?

For years after 1986, employed (dependent) children's tax returns become rather complex. Each child's income has to be distinguished between "unearned" and "earned." Unearned income by children under 14 is subject to the parent's tax rate. Earned income is subject to the child's tax rate. Children under 18 employed in a parent's business are exempt from social security tax.

Nondependent children (18 and over) file their own tax returns like any other young adult. The only difference is that if they are employed by a parent while being a full-time student away from home, there is a serious question whether any bona fide business services have been performed.

In all cases of minor and young adult children being employed by parents, *time sheets* become a requisite for documenting the actual services performed. And, of course, all employed children must use their own social security numbers.

Qualified Retirement Plans

One of the true tax benefits of owning a business is owner participation in one or more qualified retirement plans. A "qualified" plan is one which is tax qualified under the latest rules that are applicable. A business can make certain contributions to each plan and simultaneously write off those contributions as a deductible expense of the business. Such contributions are *not* included in the gross income of the owner. In addition, an owner may make limited contributions on his own, and get an immediate tax deduction for his contributions.

The feature that makes retirement plans tax attractive is the establishment of an *employee trust* for each plan. Each trust is a legal entity, somewhat like that of a corporation. It differs in that it is a tax exempt entity. It is tax exempt by virtue of the fact that all corpus (contributions and assets) and income are reserved for the exclusive benefit of the plan participants. The reserved money is not taxed until it is withdrawn from the trust by a participant or his survivor.

All qualified plans — whether pension, profit-sharing, stock bonus, deferred compensation, or other — must meet certain stringent statutory conditions. These conditions are spelled out in Sections 401 through 417 of the Internal Revenue Code. Altogether, these sections encompass approximately 90,000 words of text. Yes — 90,000 words! Section 401 alone covers some 14,000 words. Subsection 401(a), *Requirements for Qualification*, is the key introduction to all retirement plans.

The leadoff wording in Section 401(a) reads in part as—

A trust created or organized in the United States and forming part of a stock bonus, pension, or profit-sharing plan of an employer for the exclusive benefit of his employees or their beneficiaries shall constitute a qualified trust. . . .

(1) If contributions are made to the trust by such employer, or employees, or both . . .

(2) If under the trust instrument it is impossible . . . for any part of the corpus or income to be . . . used for, or diverted to, purposes other than for the exclusive benefit of his employees or their beneficiaries . . .

(3) If the plan of which such trust is a part satisfies the . . . minimum participation standards, and

(4) If the contributions or benefits provided under the plan do not discriminate in favor of employees who are:

　　(A) officers,

　　(B) shareholders, or

　　(C) highly compensated.

Altogether, there are some 25 or so requirements for qualifying a retirement plan as a tax-exempt trust. Obviously, we cannot even begin to discuss the requirements. But we can pictorialize them, as we have done in Figure 11.3. Our Figure 11.3 at least should convey the idea that another tax accountable — yet, tax deferred — entity has to be set up, administered, and maintained.

Any small business owner can set up his own retirement trust(s), so long as he provides proportionately for all nonowner employees. He can do this by adopting one or more "standardized form plans" made available by a sponsoring organization which already has received IRS approval. Various financial institutions offer these standardized plans. Most such plans have adequate flexibility for investing the retirement contributions in a prudent manner.

Annual Contribution Limits

Every business owner wants to contribute the maximum possible amount of money to his own retirement. But there are certain overall limits. For one, the maximum "compensation base" that can be taken into account is $200,000 per year. All retirement plans, in one way or another, are keyed to a participant's compensation for services rendered. This applies to owner-employees as well as to nonowner employees. For retirement plan purposes, all participating owners are automatically classed as owner-employees, regardless of the form of business.

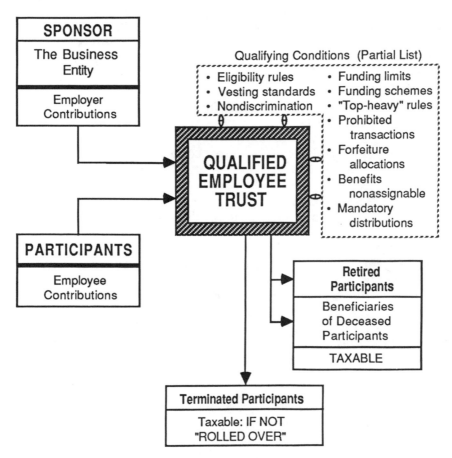

Fig. 11.3 - Features of a Business - Sponsored Retirement Plan

In the past, one of the schemes that owners used was to "long-rig" the vesting schedules of their company's retirement plans. A vesting schedule is the length of time — typically 5 to 15 years — that is required before a nonowner participant is 100% vested. If an employee was terminated short of his full vesting period, some of the employer's contributions on behalf of that employee would be forfeited. The forfeited contributions had the effect of increasing the owner's retirement benefits. Owners usually set the vesting schedules to coincide with their own interests. This is no longer possible. Today, all nonowner forfeitures are treated as employer contributions, subject to an annual limitation amount.

As per Section 415(c), the *annual addition* to a retirement plan is the sum of:

(A) employer contributions,
(B) employee contributions, and
(C) forfeitures.

The annual addition to a defined contribution plan cannot exceed **the lesser of**:

(a) $30,000 or
(b) 25 percent of the participant's compensation.

This means that if an employee contributes nothing and if there are no forfeitures, an employer can contribute up to $30,000 for each qualified participant — and deduct this amount as a current operating expense. For highly-compensated employees, this becomes a quite significant tax deduction for the business.

For defined *benefit* plans, the annual addition is based on actuarial computations that will produce yearly retirement benefits not exceeding the lesser of:

(a) $90,000 or
(b) 100 percent of the participant's average compensation for his high three years.

In such plan (defined benefit), an employee must participate for at least ten years. Hence, it is actuarially possible for an employer to contribute — and deduct — up to $90,000 for each participant year.

An employer (owner) may sponsor any number of retirement plans — of any type — that he chooses. The overall upper limit of his deductible contributions to all such plans, however, is 25% of a participant's compensation. It is conceivable, therefore, that an aggressive owner could rig his business affairs in such a way that a good portion of his own compensation was tax deferred. But this is highly unlikely. Since all employees — owners and nonowners alike — must be eligible to participate, economic and administrative reality soon sets in.

Form 5500-C/R for Each Plan

For practical reasons, the limit in number of retirement plans that a business can sustain is three. These three plans are of the following types:

1. Pension plans: fixed contributions
2. Profit-sharing plans: variable contributions
3. Other plans: elective contributions.

Each plan that is established and funded is a separate tax accountable entity on its own. This means that for each plan, an annual information return has to be filed with the IRS. The form most frequently used by small businesses is Form 5500-C/R. The official title of this form is: *Return/Report of Employee Benefit Plan (with fewer than 100 participants).* Form 5500-C/R is a six-page tax information document with approximately 200 line entries, questions, and checkboxes.

In some cases, Schedule A (Form 5500): Insurance Information, and Schedule B (Form 5500): Actuarial Information, are required attachments to Form 5500-C/R.

Schedule B (5500) is a detailed funding analysis of those contributions which an employer must make to cover persons who are:

(a) active participants,
(b) terminated participants with vested benefits, and
(c) retired participants and beneficiaries of deceased participants.

This funding analysis is made by an enrolled actuary. The required employee funding from Schedule B is compared with the actual contributions made for that year. If there is a funding deficiency, the employer must file Form 5330 (Excise Taxes Related to Employee Benefit Plans) and pay a 5% to 25% excise tax on the deficiency.

Information is also requested regarding the income and assets of each plan, each year, namely:

a. *Plan income*   _____
b. *Expenses*   _____
c. *Net income (loss)*   _____

    d.   Plan contributions   _____
    e.   Total benefits paid   _____

Total plan assets: beginning _____*; ending* _____
Total liabilities: beginning _____*; ending* _____
Net assets of plan: beginning _____*; ending* _____

Another crucial question on Form 5500-C/R is—

Does the plan satisfy the percentage tests of Code section 410(b)(1)(A)? ☐ *Yes* ☐ *No. If "No," complete worksheet in instructions and attach.*

Section 410(b)(1)(A) prescribes the minimum coverage requirements of a qualified plan. The essential statutory wording reads:

A trust shall not constitute a qualified trust under section 401(a) unless such trust is designated by the employer as part of a plan which . . . beneifts at least 70% of employees who are not highly compensated employees.

Obviously, this section is designed to prohibit an owner from stacking a plan in his sole favor.

We have intended the above to convey a subliminal message to you. The message is that the setup, funding, and maintenance of one or more retirement plans (pension, profit-sharing, or elective deferral) for yourself **and** for your employees (if any), is comprehensively complex . . . and financially draining. As a result, for a new busines starting up — whether proprietorship, partnership, or corporation — we strongly urge that you **not** engage in such plans until after three full years of profitable business operations. You have to make money first, before you can stash any of it away for retirement.

12

COMPLIANCE MATTERS

Tax Compliance For "Maximum Revenue" Is More Rigorously Enforced Today Than Ever Before. To Adapt To This Environment, You Must File On Time, Prepare A Tax Calendar, Have A "Tax Reserve," and PREPAY Your Estimated Income Taxes. In Addition, You Have Numerous Information Returns To File. The IRS Is Committed To "Total Computerization" As Its Administrative Cornerstone. This Produces Unwarranted Errors, Excessive Demands, And TCMP Intrusions Into Your Private Business And Personal Life. Access To Tax Knowledge Is Your Best Protection Against IRS Abuses.

The success of a business is independent of any taxes that it pays. In one sense, taxes can be viewed as a punishment for entering into business. In another sense, backhandedly perhaps, taxes are a measure of business success. The higher the taxes that an owner pays probably is some sort of index of his prosperity. An unsuccessful business pays little or no tax.

The problem with all taxation — federal, state, local — is that it symbolizes the presence of an "arrogant partner" in your business. This partner assumes a purely passive role in energizing and promoting the business. It contributes nothing — absolutely nothing — to its success. Yet, when profits are made, this partner asserts a dominant role in the sharing of your profits. This partner objects vehemently to sharing any of your losses.

Thus, every business starts with an arrogant tax claimant at its doorstep. Keeping this claimant at bay — while protecting yourself — is what this chapter is all about.

Vow to "File on Time"

In a new business, one is preoccupied with many matters other than taxes. There is capital to be raised; there is a product-line to be developed; there is inventory to be acquired; there is equipment to be bought and installed; there are leases of office and shop space to be signed; there are employees to be hired and trained; there are suppliers to be contacted; there are lines of credit to be arranged; there are clients and customers to be solicited; there is a marketing strategy to be pursued; there is advertising and promotional literature to be prepared; there is a sales staff to be motivated . . . and on and on. In this environment, it is easy to ignore all tax concerns.

This explains the most common oversight of every new business. The owner postpones filing his applicable tax forms. Sometimes the postponement is made official by "applying for an extension." But, more often, the postponement is undertaken unilaterally. The owner rationalizes that: "I'm just getting started. The 'government' ought to understand that I can't do everything at once. I'll get to the tax filings in due course."

One postponement leads to another which, in turn, leads to still another postponement. Before it is realized, bad habits set in. Late tax filings become the rule, rather than the exception.

It takes up to 18 months for government workers to process a tax filing. Thus, if your filing is late, you are not pounced on immediately. This can give you a sense of false security. You may conclude, erroneously, that the government understands your situation.

Tax agencies — the IRS, state, and local — do *not* understand the trials and tribulations of starting a business. Furthermore, they do not care. They are not the least bit interested in your problems. They are tax *collectors* . . . and that's all they are.

You are getting the point, aren't you?

The point is that you should vow to yourself to always file on time. *File on time—no matter what!*

If your timely filing is not 100% correct, you can amend it later (no penalty). An incorrect return filed on time is less apt to be brandished by the system, than a correct return filed late.

Even if you file a blank form, file it on time. Often when first starting a business, there is little or no computational data on which the tax can be determined. Yet, some tax filing date is at hand. If this happens to you, file the applicable form on time . . . in blank. Write in bold red letters at the top right-hand edge:

NEW BUSINESS; NO INCOME THIS PERIOD
or
NEW BUSINESS; NO EMPLOYEES THIS PERIOD.

Establish A Tax Calendar

The scheduling of periodic activities is commonplace in business. There are employees to be paid; there are suppliers to be paid; there are accounts receivable to be reminded; there are business appointments to be made; there are promotional releases, sales campaigns, and other events to be scheduled. So, why not schedule your tax filing events? Why not establish and maintain a "tax calendar"?

The nature of one's business determines the number and frequency of tax forms that have to be filed. Consequently, each business entity — and each owner individually — needs to tailor its/his tax calendar to the specific business at hand. There is no standard tax calendar for all businesses. Your calendar should be set up on a full-year basis, with all due dates clearly identified thereon.

There are various tax forms to file at different times during the year. There are income taxes, estimated taxes (on income), social security taxes, medicare taxes, state unemployment taxes, sales taxes, excise taxes, property taxes, business licenses, vehicle licenses. Have we missed any?

Most tax forms are accompanied by instructions which designate the due dates and the "mail to" address of the agency involved. We suggest that you categorize all of the tax forms that are applicable to your business, and make appropriate notations on your tax calendar.

Try to discipline yourself to have the tax forms prepared and mailed 10 days before the actual due dates. This allows adequate time for postal foulups and incoming stackups at the tax agency involved. All tax agencies stamp on your forms the date that they receive them. They make no attempt whatever to record the date that you mailed them. So, you need five to ten days leeway.

If you are one of those persons who waits until the very last minute to file, we suggest that you send your tax forms by *certified mail*. Officially, a tax form is filed when you deposit it in the U.S. Postal system. If you do this on the due date, you have no way of proving that you indeed mailed it on time. If you are assessed a late penalty because the tax agency received it after the due date, what do you do?

You photocopy the post-office stamped certified mail receipt, send it to the tax agency, and challenge the late penalty.

Have Access to a "Tax Reserve"

Most small businesses are chronically short of cash. While the tax forms themselves may be prepared on time, the money often is not on hand to make the tax payments on time. More likely than not, the money is tied up in accounts receivable or in unsold inventory.

The temptation in these circumstances is to wait a few weeks in the hope of collecting money from those who owe you. Though you know you will be filing late, at least you'll be able to pay the full amount of tax due.

Resist such temptation. In the first place, you'd be violating your own "file on time" vow. In the second place, you have no assurance that the receivable money will come in when you expect it. Never count on money that a customer or client assures you: "It's in the mail."

Always protect yourself with a *tax reserve*. This can be a personal savings account of your own. It can be a business savings account. It can be in informal line-of-credit with family members and friends, or a formal line-of-credit with a commercial lending institution. It is better to borrow money at commercial interest rates to pay taxes on time than to pay taxes late. The late penalties could horrify you.

Some cash-short taxpayers take the position that they will file on time, make a token payment in good faith, and attach a note explaining why the payment is not in full. And, sometimes, they request the tax agency to help them arrange a "payment schedule."

Before any payment schedule can be arranged, the tax agency will insist that you fill out a comprehensive financial disclosure statement. You will be asked to describe and value your assets, tell exactly where they are located, and give exact account, license, and serial numbers. More frequently than not, this statement is used —

particularly by the IRS — for SEIZING your assets rather than for arranging a payment schedule. Many a well-meaning taxpayer has been shocked and dismayed by the "behind your back" tactics that tax agencies will use. Seized assets are tax sold way below their fair market value.

If you are in a trade or business of any kind, no tax agency is going to be sympathetic to your inability to make full payment when due. So, don't ask for any sympathy. Don't ask for any payment schedule either. File on time and pay as much as you can. The tax agency will then bill you for the "balance due" . . . which will include penalties and interest.

Prepaying Income Tax

All tax payments except income taxes (business and personal) are payable at the time the tax forms are due-date filed. As to income taxes, special *prepayment installments* have to be made. Although an income tax return itself is due once a year, installment prepayments of the estimated tax are due four times a year. This presents a tax planning problem.

Most business owners object to prepaying income tax, until they know what their net income is for the year. They argue against the entire concept of any prepayment of estimates. In small businesses, the net income is seldom uniform from year to year. There are good years and bad years; there are many uncertainties in between. When told that they are expected to prepay 90% of the final tax due, *before* the final tax is computed, the injustice can cause emotions to erupt.

There is an estimated income tax law for individuals, proprietorships, and partnerships (Sec. 6654), and a separate such law for corporations (Sec. 6655). In principal part, these estimation laws state that—

> *The amount of any required installment shall be 25 percent of the required annual payment* . . . [meaning] *the lesser of—*
> *(i) 90 percent of the tax shown on the return for the taxable year, or*
> *(ii) 100 percent* [or 110 percent] *of the tax shown on the return . . . for the preceding taxable year* . . . [as applicable].

There is, of course, a penalty (called: *underpayment* penalty) for not making an estimated prepayment, or for not making it on time. This means that there is a potential of four penalties per year! Each penalty, however, is not all that severe. It is the equivalent of lost interest to the government for tax money not received.

There are two due-date schedules for making the four prepayment installments. These are:

	Calendar Year	Fiscal Year
1st	April 15	15th day of 4th month
2nd	June 15	15th day of 6th month
3rd	Sept. 15	15th day of 9th month
4th	Jan. 15	15th day of 12th month

If the 15th day falls on Saturday, Sunday, or a legal holiday, the next regular business day is the due date.

For individuals (including proprietorships and partnerships) the estimated payments are made on Form 1040-ES (called: *Payment Vouchers*). For corporations, the payments are made on Form 8109 (called: *Deposit Coupons*). These are federal form numbers. Most states have corresponding forms for prepayments of the state tax.

It is too complicated to try to explain the 90% rule for estimating your pretax. Our suggestions is that you guess the best that you can, using your preceding year's tax as a reference. This is the 100% rule above. If business looks good, guess up; if business looks bad, guess down. If you guess wrong, the underpayment penalty is not devastating (less than 1% per month).

Filing of Information Returns

Not all tax forms that you file involve the payment of tax by you. There are numerous other forms which are simply *information* returns. That is, you report certain information so that the IRS (and state tax agencies) can computer-check on the recipients of that information. The information reported is a specific dollar amount on which there may be a tax due by the recipient.

In a cynical way, you are forced into being a tax spy for government. We say "forced" because there are penalties on you for not reporting or not reporting correctly. If you don't file an information return when you should have, there is a $50 penalty for each failure. If you file, but omit correct information or report incorrect information, there is a $5 penalty for each omission or each incorrection. Philosophically, one has to wonder about our free enterprise system.

Altogether, for all types of businesses, there are some 20 to 25 information returns prescribed. Not all information forms are applicable to an ordinary trade or business. Large financial institutions, brokerage houses, international corporations, foreign trusts, government agencies, and gambling casinos will use forms that you will not likely use. We think that as many as 10 or so information returns could be applicable when starting and operating a modest-size business.

Rather than trying to explain each of the information returns that could be applicable to you, we list and briefly describe them in Figure 12.1. Do note that Form 8300 has to be filed within 15 days of your receiving any cash payments over $10,000. You have more time for the other forms listed.

With the exception of Forms 5500C/R (retirement plan) and 8308 (partnership interests), a copy of each information return must be submitted to each recipient 30 days after the end of each calendar year. And 30 days later, the returns have to be filed with the IRS (and with corresponding state agencies). Form 8308 is filed on April 15th and Form 5500C/R is filed on July 31st. All of these filings re-emphasize the importance of a tax calendar.

Resolving "Computer Tyranny"

The IRS is totally committed to computer processing and optical scanning of all tax returns, tax payments, and information forms submitted to it. No human being reads — or cares to read — the mountains of pieces of paper and magnetic blips that pour in. New tax laws mean more tax forms and more magnetic media reportings. A stony bureaucratic monster has been created. In one sense, it is a marvel that the tax collection system works at all.

There are times — discouragingly often — when the system does *not* work as it is supposed to. When it doesn't work, the result is outright computer tyranny. When there is a mixup, an avalanche of computer demands, miscomputations, and penalty assertions gush forth. The trigger mechanism may be a one-cent arithmetic error, a one-letter misspelling of a name, a one-digit transposition of a number, or a one-line misentry on a form. When the computer avalanche starts, a taxpayer is devastated before he can get the attention of an IRS human to turn the robot off.

Let us cite a real life recent case. A new business starter (wife) filed Form SS-4: Application for Employer Identification Number. She indicated that she was in partnership with her husband, in a

FORM	TITLE	PURPOSE
1098	Mortgage Interest Statement	To report $600 or more of mortgage interest received
1099 - A	Abandonment of Secured Property	Acquisition or abandonment property as security for debt
1099 - B	Barter & Securities Transactions	Amounts bartered; stock sales; mutual fund redemptions
1099 - C	Cancellation of debt	Treated as taxable income to debtor
1099 - DIV	Dividends Statement	Dividend payments of $10 or more; distributions $600 or more
1099 - INT	Interest Statement	To report $10 or more of interest paid to others
1099 - MISC	Nonemployee & Other Payments	$600 or more paid for rents, royalties, prizes, awards, services
1099 - R	Retirement Plan Distributions	Distributions to employees from pension & profit sharing plans
1099 - S	Sales of Real Estate	By brokers & escrow agents processing sales of realty
5500 - C/R	Employee Benefit Plan	Return / report on plans with fewer than 100 participants
8300	Cash Payments Over $10,000	Filed within 15 days of receipt in trade or business
8308	Sale or Exchange of Partnership Interest	To report any changes in ownership interest & property
W - 2	Wage & Tax Statement	Gross wages, bonuses, fringe benefits, & withholdings

Fig. 12.1 - Information Returns Applicable to Small Business

business which started in 1986. She also indicated that she would have several employees.

The IRS computer operator punched in 1966 . . . instead of 1986. Then the IRS computer-directed forms center shipped to the applicant *20 years* of Form 1065 (for partnerships), 20 years of Form 1040 (for individuals), 20 years (*80 quarters*) of Form 941 (employer taxes), and 20 years of Form 940 (federal unemployment tax). Altogether, 140 different tax forms! Each form consisted of multiple pages with instructions. They all arrived in four cartons, each 10"(W)x12"(L)x8"(H).

Before the taxpayer could open all four cartons, 140 separate IRS envelopes arrived, each containing a computer demand. In addition to demanding that each form be filed immediately, late penalties and negligence penalties were cited, all followed by threats of seizing the taxpayer's assets for noncompliance. Needless to say, the taxpayer was furious.

How would *you* handle a computer avalanche like this?

In every IRS District, there is a Problem Resolution Office. It is manned — or womanned — by one or two actual human beings. The sole function of this office is to intercept, intercede, investigate, and correct the inevitable computer foulups by the IRS. The persons there have no authority to interpret tax law, nor to make tax decisions, nor to instruct on tax filings. Their role is to resolve problems that computers create. If you have a genuine problem in this regard, the problem resolution persons can be very helpful. When the need arises, use them.

Subjection to TCMP Audit

In order to make the computer system more revenue productive, the IRS conducts intensive in-depth audits of selected taxpayers. These are special audits. By targeting "representative taxpayers," statistical data is collected on the nature and extent of their compliance with the tax laws. This data is used to retune and refine the discriminant function scoring of all returns processed through IRS National Computer Center (at Martinsburg, West Virginia).

This special statistical sampling is called: TCMP audit. The letters TCMP mean — **Total Compliance Measurement Program.** The phrase "total compliance" says it all. Such compliance can only be measured by an exhaustive line-by-line examination of *every item* on a tax return.

Small businesses are natural targets for TCMP statistics. They represent a good cross-section of national business activities involving diverse tax laws. Small business owners are productive individuals. They are generalists in broad areas of the business. Thus, IRS agents can interview fewer (knowledgeable) individuals and get access to widespread tax compliance information. There would be difficulty in accessing the same type of information in highly-departmentalized large business entities. Sooner or later, many a small business will be subjected to a TCMP audit.

A TCMP audit is a scrutinizing and agonizing experience. All pretense of reasonableness and probable cause are thrown to the wind. Nothing is taken for granted. Nothing is taken on testimony. There is no compromise. An item is either all black or all white. Every line entry on the return — including all supporting schedules and related returns — must be supported by valid documentation. This applies to every item of income, every expense, every deduction, every allowance, every adjustment, and every credit. All bank accounts, savings accounts, and investment accounts are examined. A TCMP audit can easily span three to six months of your business time. The additional revenue produced may only be $100. The amount of revenue doesn't matter; statistics do. This is clearly a situation where the IRS is over-reaching its statutory authority.

Two federal appeals courts have held that a taxpayer can refuse to open himself up to a TCMP audit. [*U.S. v. Flagg* (1980, CA8) 634 F2d 1087; *U.S. v. Bank of Dallas* (1981, CA5) 635 F2d 391.] Ignoring the courts, the IRS turned around and sent a Notice of Deficiency to each of the refusing taxpayers. The Notice arbitrarily disallowed all adjustments, all deductions, and all credits on the returns. Tax was assessed solely on the total gross income on each return. A Notice of Deficiency gives a taxpayer up to 90 days in which to pay the assessed tax, petition to Tax Court, or allow his assets to be seized.

When confronted with a TCMP audit notice, a business owner faces a dilemma. Just how much compulsory intrusion into his private business affairs and private life does he allow? A "selectee" wants to cooperate, but he also wants his constitutional rights protected. If he cooperates, can he be assured that the IRS will respect his rights? An overview of the *exposure factors* that a business owner faces (in his dilemma) is presented in Figure 12.2. As the right-portion of this figure indicates, a cooperative taxpayer never knows what the IRS will use against him.

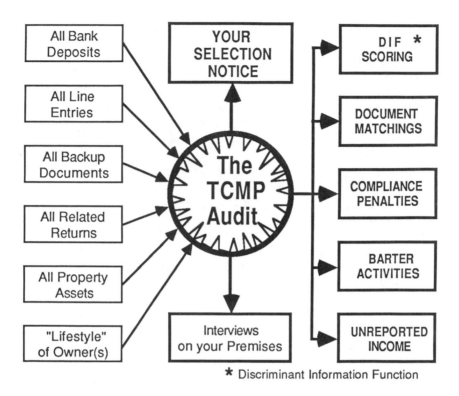

* Discriminant Information Function

Fig. 12.2 - The Compulsion / Intrusion Role of TCMP Audits

Beware of IRS Abuses

Because there are so many tax laws, there has evolved a presumption that the IRS is correct in its interpretation of those laws. This presumption of correctness is a *theory of convenience* only. It would be impractical to collect taxes if the IRS had to prove its position in every instance. A certain amount of interpretive discretion has to be allowed that agency. Otherwise, government would come to a halt due to its inability to collect needed revenue.

The presumption of correctness by the IRS is an *initial* position only. It is not prima facie evidence. The presumption falls when a taxpayer presents competent evidence and authority that would support a contrary interpretation on the issue. The issue is then decided on the basis of evidence presented by both the taxpayer and the IRS, without consideration of the presumption. [*Griffin v. Com.*, 285 F2d 91; *Niederkrome v. Com.*, 266 F2d 238.]

Much too often, the IRS abuses its interpretive discretion. It does this by ignoring the legislative intent of a law, and makes that interpretation which produces maximum revenue. It does this arbitrarily, regardless of what the law says or even what IRS's own regulations say. By so doing, the taxpayer — under the presumption theory — is forced into the position of having to prove the IRS wrong. Even on those issues where the IRS knows it is wrong, it acts the way it does because it knows that 98% of the taxpayers will concede and give in.

Let us exemplify this abuse in a situation which affects many small businesses. Consider Sections 174(a) and 263A of the Internal Revenue Code. Section 174(a) deals with the research and development of new products and services which may be current expensed rather than capitalized. Section 263A(a) deals with the capitalization of those tangible property items produced by the taxpayer. Subsection 263A(c)(2) specifically excludes Section 174(a) from the capitalization requirements.

The IRS takes the position that if one is engaged in a trade or business, any new product or new service that is developed in connection with that trade or business must be capitalized. It asserts that Section 263A applies. This assertion is directly contrary to Section 174(a) which says that—

A taxpayer may treat research or experimental expenditures . . . as expenses which are not chargeable to capital account.

The IRS strong-arms businesses into the capitalization route because it generates more tax revenue. The current expense route is more beneficial to the taxpayer.

Our position is that you cannot trust the IRS to make the right interpretation of the tax laws. It insists on ignoring the intent of Congress, if it can find another law to assert as applicable. This arbitrary attitude is a clear abuse of its discretion. We caution you, therefore, to be on-alert for IRS abuses and be prepared to stand your ground.

Adapting and Thriving

Anyone in business these days will have to adapt to more rigorous tax compliance enforcement than ever before. This has come about because of a fundamental change in tax philosophy enacted in 1982. Instead of collecting only the correct tax, the

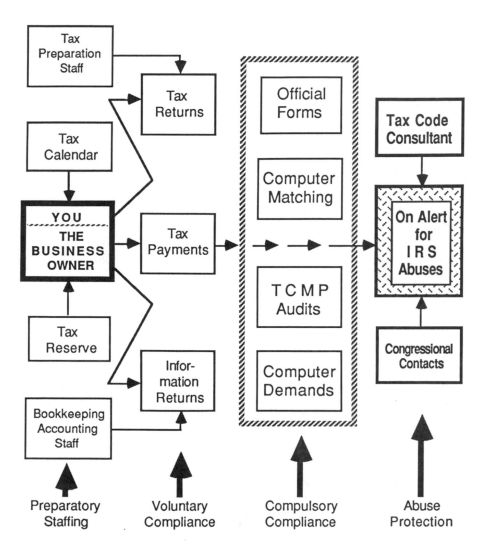

Fig. 12.3 - Summary of Tax Compliance Functions in Business

emphasis now is on collecting maximum revenue. This new enforcement policy is called: Tax Equity and Fiscal Responsibility (TEFRA). Because of the greater amount of gross income per return, more revenue can be collected from businesses than from individuals.

By adapting to a rigorous tax environment, you can actually thrive in business. This is not because paying taxes and filing forms is going to make you more profitable. It is because your competitors and others in business will be facing the same rigorous compliance procedures. If you adapt and they don't, you'll have more constructive time to devote to your business. Nonadaptees will spend many wasted hours responding to compliance demands. Dealing with tax agents and their arbitrariness is dissatisfying.

An overall summary of the compliance matters facing business is presented in Figure 12.3. Most of the items shown have been discussed previously. There are two new items that we want to make comment on, in closing this chapter (and book).

Because of the diversity of tax laws applicable to business, every business owner should have a qualified tax consultant on tap. Times and situations will arise when you will need special research into the federal tax code, regulations, and court decisions of the past. For this, you should have ready access to a specialist who is independent from your own staff. You need this as *abuse protection* — somewhat like insurance. In its eagerness to maximize revenue, the IRS and its agents will frequently overreach. An independent researcher can review the authorities on point to help you counter the IRS positions.

Another tool in your abuse protection plan is contact with your local Congressman's office. Every Congressman has a member of his staff who is an "IRS contact." This person has direct access to the IRS District Office in your business area. You can make complaints to your Congressman's office where, in turn, direct inquiry can be made on your behalf. A single Congressman cannot do much about the tax laws or the computation of your taxes. However, his intervention on your behalf sometimes can induce the IRS to be more reasonable.

In closing, we want to restate a harsh environmental fact. Today, federal tax collection focuses on the *extraction of maximum revenue* (tax, plus penalties, plus interest) from businesses . . . and from their owners. To survive in this environment, you must manage your tax affairs diligently. You can do it!

ABOUT
THE AUTHOR

Holmes F. Crouch

Born on a small farm in southern Maryland, Holmes was graduated from the U.S. Coast Guard Academy with a Bachelor's Degree in Marine Engineering. While serving on active duty, he wrote many technical articles on maritime matters. After attaining the rank of Lieutenant Commander, he resigned to pursue a career as a nuclear engineer.

Continuing his education, he earned a Master's Degree in Nuclear Engineering from the University of California. He also authored two books on nuclear propulsion. As a result of the tax write-offs associated with writing these books, the IRS audited his returns. The IRS's handling of the audit procedure so annoyed Holmes that he undertook to become as knowledgeable as possible regarding tax procedures. He became a licensed private Tax Practitioner by passing an examination administered by the IRS. Having attained this credential, he started his own tax preparation and counseling business in 1972.

In the early years of his tax practice, he was a regular talk-show guest on San Francisco's KGO Radio responding to hundreds of phone-in tax questions from listeners. He was a much sought-after guest speaker at many business seminars and taxpayer meetings. He also provided counseling on special tax problems, such as divorce matters, property exchanges, timber harvesting, mining ventures, animal breeding, independent contractors, selling businesses, and offices-at-home. Over the past 25 years, he has prepared nearly 10,000 tax returns for individuals, estates, trusts, and small businesses (in partnership and corporate form).

During the tax season of January through April, he prepares returns in a unique manner. During a single meeting, he completes the return . . . *on the spot!* The client leaves with his return signed, sealed, and in a stamped envelope. His unique approach to preparing returns and his personal interest in his clients' tax affairs have honed his professional proficiency. His expertise extends through itemized deductions, computer-matching of income sources, capital gains and losses, business expenses and cost of goods, residential rental expenses, limited and general partnership activities, closely-held corporations, to family farms and ranches.

He remembers spending 12 straight hours completing a doctor's complex return. The next year, the doctor, having moved away, utilized a large accounting firm to prepare his return. Their accountant was so impressed by the manner in which the prior return was prepared that he recommended the doctor travel the 500 miles each year to have Holmes continue doing it.

He recalls preparing a return for an unemployed welder, for which he charged no fee. Two years later the welder came back and had his return prepared. He paid the regular fee . . . and then added a $300 tip.

During the off season, he represents clients at IRS audits and appeals. In one case a shoe salesman's audit was scheduled to last three hours. However, after examining Holmes' documentation it was concluded in 15 minutes with "no change" to his return. In another instance he went to an audit of a custom jeweler that the IRS dragged out for more than six hours. But, supported by Holmes' documentation, the client's return was accepted by the IRS with "no change."

Then there was the audit of a language translator that lasted two full days. The auditor scrutinized more than $1.25 million in gross receipts, all direct costs, and operating expenses. Even though all expensed items were documented and verified, the auditor decided that more than $23,000 of expenses ought to be listed as capital items for depreciation instead. If this had been enforced it would have resulted in a significant additional amount of tax. Holmes strongly disagreed and after many hours explanation got the amount reduced by more than 60% on behalf of his client.

He has dealt extensively with gift, death and trust tax returns. These preparations have involved him in the tax aspects of wills, estate planning, trustee duties, probate, marital and charitable bequests, gift and death exemptions, and property titling.

Although not an attorney, he prepares Petitions to the U.S. Tax Court for clients. He details the IRS errors and taxpayer facts by citing pertinent sections of tax law and regulations. In a recent case involving an attorney's ex-spouse, the IRS asserted a tax deficiency of $155,000. On behalf of his client, he petitioned the Tax Court and within six months the IRS conceded the case.

Over the years, Holmes has observed that the IRS is not the industrious, impartial, and competent federal agency that its official public imaging would have us believe.

He found that, at times, under the slightest pretext, the IRS has interpreted against a taxpayer in order to assess maximum penalties, and may even delay pending matters so as to increase interest due on additional taxes. He has confronted the IRS in his own behalf on five separate occasions, going before the U.S. Claims Court, U.S. District Court, and U.S. Tax Court. These were court actions that tested specific sections of the Internal Revenue Code which he found ambiguous, inequitable, and abusively interpreted by the IRS.

Disturbed by the conduct of the IRS and by the general lack of tax knowledge by most individuals, he began an innovative series of taxpayer-oriented Federal tax guides. To fulfill this need, he undertook the writing of a series of guidebooks that provide in-depth knowledge on one tax subject at a time. He focuses on subjects that plague taxpayers all throughout the year. Hence, his formulation of the "Allyear" Tax Guide series.

The author is indebted to his wife, Irma Jean, and daughter, Barbara MacRae, for the word processing and computer graphics that turn his experiences into the reality of these publications. Holmes welcomes comments, questions, and suggestions from his readers. He can be contacted in California at (408) 867-2628, or by writing to the publisher's address.

ALLYEAR Tax Guides
by Holmes F. Crouch

All of the above available at bookstores, libraries, and on the internet

For a free 8-page catalog,
or information about the above titles, contact:
ALLYEAR Tax Guides
20484 Glen Brae Drive, Saratoga, CA 95070
Phone: (408) 867-2628   Fax: (408) 867-6466